[illegible] TO BIRDS OF THE NORTHERN HEMISPHERE

THE POCKET GUIDE TO

SEABIRDS OF THE NORTHERN HEMISPHERE

ALAN RICHARDS

DRAGON'S WORLD

Dragon's World Ltd
Limpsfield
Surrey RH8 0DY
Great Britain

First published by Dragon's World Ltd 1992

Editor: Diana Steedman
Designer and Series Design: Dave Allen
Editorial Director: Pippa Rubinstein

The catalogue record for this book is available from the British Library.

ISBN 1 85028 147 5

Typeset by Tradespools Ltd., Frome, Somerset

Printed in Singapore

Contents

Introduction

Nearly three quarters of the earth's surface is covered by ocean, in which a multiplicity of creatures exists, from microscopic plankton to the largest living mammals, the whales. A complex food chain not only sustains this marine environment but provides support for life forms that do not actually live in that domain. Many birds find the sea and its environs an unending food source, living from the abundance of fish found in it, though never depleting this resource.

True seabirds are those whose usual habitat is the sea, it being their primary source of food. They are amongst the most numerous of birds in global terms, some species being numbered in their millions. Their noise and grace are familiar to us from seaside holidays but what may not be realized is that many of these beautiful and exciting birds will have flown thousands of miles to breed on our coastlines. The Arctic Tern, for example, is capable of journeys of over 12,000 miles between its wintering and breeding areas.

The following family groups breed around the coasts of Britain and western Europe, occur as non-breeding visitors to all or some of these areas, or have their breeding grounds on the Atlantic coasts of North America. It is from these groups that a selection has been made for this guide.

Albatrosses	Diomedeidae
Petrels and shearwaters	Procellariidae
Storm Petrels	Hydrobatidae
Gannets and Boobies	Sulidae
Cormorants	Phalacrocoracidae
Pelicans	Pelecanidae
Skuas	Stercorariidae
Gulls	Laridae
Terns and Noddies	Sternidae
Skimmers	Rynchopidae
Auks	Alcidae

They are to be found in three main sea zones:

Inshore, shallow sea areas: this zone is used by such species as cormorants, pelicans, gulls, some terns and the skimmers.

Offshore (but not far from the coast): this is the feeding area for gannets, boobies and the auks, but also some terns and gulls.

Open sea (many miles from land): this is the domain of the truly oceanic or pelagic species: the albatrosses, petrels, shearwaters, storm-petrels, skuas and kittiwakes.

Our ability to recognize birds is not helped by the conditions under which observation may take place, but a series of key

characters will certainly help with identification. These are:
Field marks: noting the body shape, the wings' shape and positioning, the tail shape and especially the size and shape of the bill, will enable the birdwatcher to at least categorize its grouping; the colour of the legs and bill will then help with further distinction.
Plumage: wing patterns are important and whilst there are rarely plumage differences between males and females in seabirds, some species do have definite breeding and non-breeding plumages. Normally a complete moult occurs before and after breeding, so it is important to note that non-breeding (winter) plumage will differ from that of breeding (summer) plumage. The photographs in this guide depict adult birds in breeding plumage, but many species undergo several plumage changes as full maturity is attained.
Feeding behaviour is another identification aid: cormorants dive from the surface; skuas will harass and rob other birds; gannets plunge head first into the sea from some height; whilst gulls flock to waste tips.
Distribution: very little is understood of the pelagic species' migration and dispersal. The maps indicate in three shades migration ranges (light blue), extent of breeding range (mid-blue), breeding locations (dark blue).

There are many other bird species whose life is also dependent upon the sea, though not totally. Particularly during the breeding season these 'secondary' seabirds may be found in the vicinity of lakes, rivers and marshes, often many miles from the sea. They comprise the divers (Gaviidae), grebes (Podicipedidae), some wildfowl (Anatidae), and possibly most wading birds can be included in this category. These family groups are not included in this book but in *The Pocket Guide to Shorebirds of the Northern Hemisphere*, and *The Pocket Guide to Ducks of Britain and the Northern Hemisphere* (Dragon's World).

To watch seabirds in their sea environment, a boat trip really becomes a necessary excursion. This has been a popular birdwatching activity off the west coast of the USA for some years now and is gaining popularity in Britain. Whether a sea trip is a North Sea ferry crossing, a boat trip around the Farne Islands, or a visit to the Isles of Scilly, the expectation, excitement and thrill of watching seabirds will never diminish.

KEY TO MAPS

- breeding area
- range during breeding season
- migration and winter range

Black-browed Albatross

Diomedea melanophris 83–93cm (31½–36½in)

Nest	A pile of locally obtained vegetation
Egg clutch	One
Egg colour	White
Laid	October
Incubation	70 days
Fledging	120 days

Identification An extremely large bird, much bigger than a Gannet, it has the appearance of an outsize Fulmar.

The body is stout, the wings are long and narrow (wingspan 2m (6ft) and typical of an albatross) providing a characteristic continuous powerful gliding flight, usually low over the waves. The adult Black-browed Albatross has a white head and neck with white underparts and white rump which contrast with the dark back, tail and upperwing surfaces; the underwing shows a narrow white strip with dark margins to the leading and trailing edges. Many birds show white axillaries, though they are variable

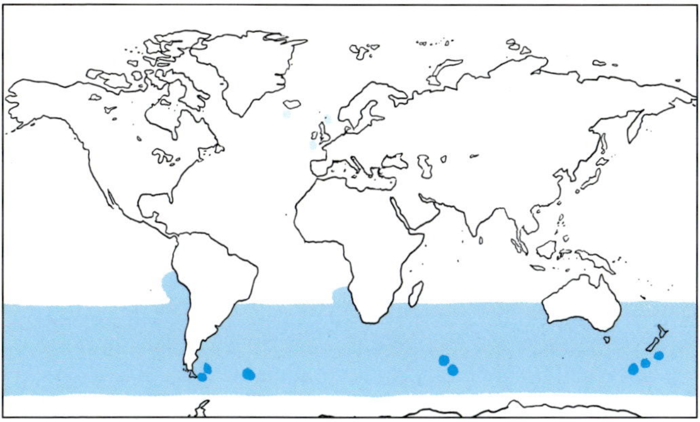

and some are a less distinctive dusky-grey. Close views of an adult will reveal the dark eyebrows, which extend as a short narrow streak through and behind the eye, giving the bird a frowning expression. The large, hooked bill is pinkish yellow. The immature bird has a grey head and neck, with a dark, or horn-coloured, bill. The sexes are similar and there are no seasonal variations. There are similarities which need to be considered between this species and the Yellow-nosed Albatross (*Diomedea chlororhynchos*) and Grey-headed Albatross (*D. chrysostoma*) which need to be considered, but only where ranges overlap in the southern hemisphere.
Voice Mainly silent at sea, but utters croaking calls during courtship.
Habitat Nests on remote rocky islands, at other times pelagic.
Food Regularly follows ships and feeds at trawler guttings. Squid and fish.
Range Breeds southern oceans on islands of Cape Horn, Staten Island, Ildefonso Island, South Georgia, Falkland Islands, Kerguelen, Heard Island, Macquarie Island, Campbell Island and Antipodes Island.
Movements Returns to nesting colonies from end of September. Young birds disperse the following April after fledging and move to nearby coasts of either South America or New Zealand and Australian waters. Adults tend to migrate northwards over the open seas of the Tropics. Occasionally strays into northern hemisphere.

One bird frequented Bass Rock in the summers of 1967–69; another, possibly the same, has returned to Hermaness in Unst, Shetland, since 1972. There have been a number of other sightings of passing birds around Britain, mainly April to May and July to early November.

Fulmar

Fulmarus glacialis 45–51cm (18–20in)

Nest Bare rock or shallow depression. When on soft soil a few small stones sometimes added
Egg clutch One
Egg colour White
Laid May
Incubation 52–53 days
Fledging 46 days

Identification A gull-like bird appearing grey and white at a distance, but unlike gulls, has no black in wings or white in tail. In the air, cruciform shape suggests 'Shearwater' species or small albatross, especially when it banks and glides in stiff-winged

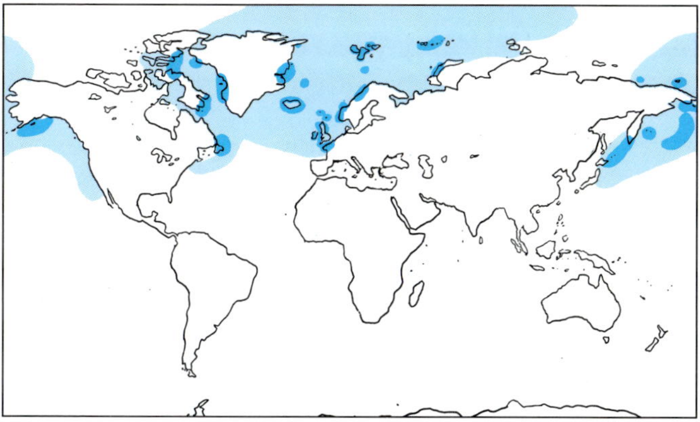

flight just above waves. The head, neck and underparts are ivory white and the back, wings and tail are bluish grey. The bill is greenish brown, parts of which are tinged blue and pink and the blunt-hooked tip is brownish horn. External tube-like nostrils are a shared characteristic of albatrosses, shearwaters and petrels. The legs are greenish grey. The dark eye is emphasized by a small patch of dark feathers in front of the socket. There are both light and dark morphs of this bird. The Northern Fulmar or Blue Fulmar is the darkest, being uniform smoke-grey. This is found predominantly within the Pacific range where intermediates of all shades occur. The light morphs predominate in the Atlantic where dark morphs are rare.

Voice Cackling noises and crooning notes at nest, silent at other times.

Habitat Prefers narrow ledges on precipitous sea cliffs for nesting, but also uses low earthbanks, crevices in rocks, and unused stone buildings. At other times found way out to sea.

Food Fish, fish offal, crustaceans, cephalopods and any fish or mammalian carrion seized from surface of the water.

Range Found throughout the high Arctic of the North Atlantic including Baffin Island, north-east Greenland, Spitsbergen, Bear Island, Franz Josef Land. Also north-west Greenland, Newfoundland, Jan Mayen, Iceland, Faeroes, British Isles (nesting on all suitable sites around the entire coast), Commander Islands and France.

Movements After breeding, disperses over the sea, leaving inshore waters from August through to October during main period of moult.

The Fulmar glides over the sea, revealing its diagnostic cruciform shape and stiff-winged flight pattern.

Cory's Shearwater

Calonectris diomedea 46–53cm (18–21in)

Nest	In cavity at end of tunnel in soft soil, or natural hole in rocks. Small stones or pieces of shell might form lining
Egg clutch	One
Egg colour	White and glossy
Laid	April
Incubation	53 days
Fledging	Up to 85 days

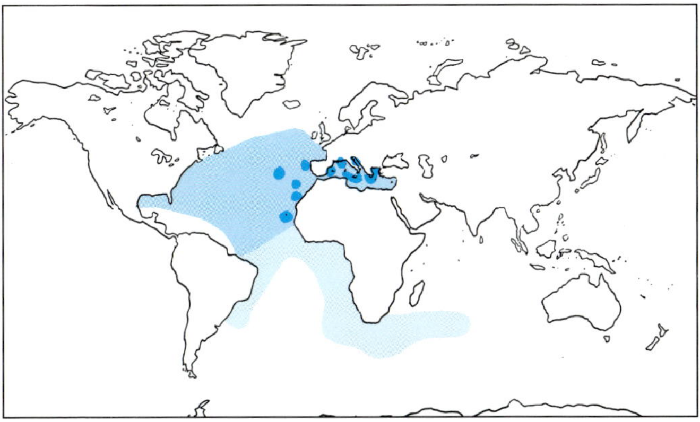

Identification About same size as the Great Shearwater but lacking any marked features of that species, the greyish brown upperparts merge into white underparts without any sharp contrast. The underwing is mostly white with narrow brownish margins with dark wing tips. The flight is more leisurely and buoyant than other shearwaters with the broad wings held looser and flexed showing a characteristic bowing especially noticeable front-on. Regularly feeds on the wing, skimming over surface and dipping or making shallow dives. The yellow bill is quite noticeable even at fairly long range. Follows ships and is attracted to trawler catches. The sexes are alike and there is no seasonal variation.
Voice Silent at sea, but noisy at nest sites, uttering harsh rasping notes.
Habitat Nests on rocky islands, frequenting inshore waters, but ranges far out to sea in mainly warm waters from temperate to sub-tropical regions.
Food Chiefly fish, cephalopods and crustaceans, also scavenges offal thrown from fishing vessels.
Range Breeds Mediterranean Islands, also Azores and Cape Verde Islands, Madeira group, and Canaries.
Movements Returns to nest sites from late February when large numbers can be seen passing Strait of Gibraltar. Many can also be observed during post-breeding dispersal October/November. Periodically occurs in exceptional numbers round Britain, otherwise scattered occurrences, mainly August. Most frequently noted Cornwall and south-west Ireland.

A scarce visitor to British waters, Cory's Shearwaters occur in small numbers during migrations. It is more often seen in the Mediterranean.

Great Shearwater

Puffinus gravis 48cm (19in)

Nest	In underground burrows or grass tussocks
Egg clutch	One
Egg colour	White
Laid	Not known
Incubation	September
Fledging	Not known

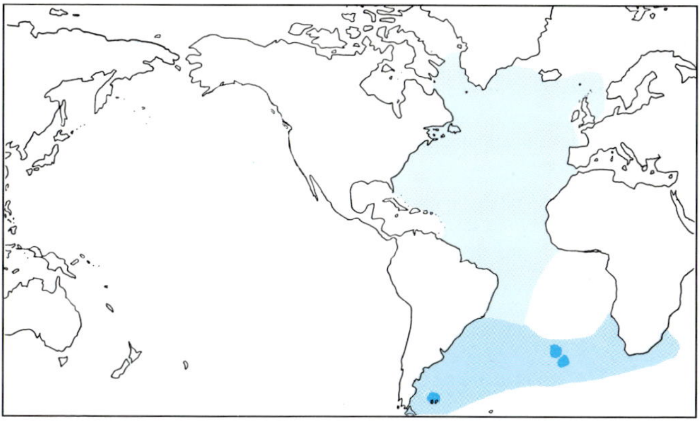

Identification A large shearwater, its dark brown cap, white cheeks, white nape, contrasting with greyish-brown upperparts should readily distinguish the species, while the white underparts which show a dark belly patch (though this is often difficult to detect out over the sea) are a diagnostic feature. Also the rump usually shows a narrow white horse-shoe-shaped patch. Wings less bowed than Cory's Shearwater, with flight strong and direct with quick wing beats. Feeds by plunge diving from 6–10m (20–33ft) above surface of water, but also dives from swimming position. Attends trawlers in numbers when noisy and aggressive. Sexes are similar and there is no seasonal variation.
Voice Makes sounds like fighting cats when squabbling over food.
Habitat Nests on rocky islands, otherwise totally pelagic.
Food Mainly fish and cephalopods. Also scavenges fish catches.
Range Nests in South Atlantic at three main breeding sites: Nightingale Island, Inaccessible Island of Tristan da Cunha and Gough Island. Oceanic in cold to fairly cold waters.
Movements Returns to breeding areas September onwards. Young disperse following May. Adults begin trans-equatorial migration across Atlantic in April, moving north-west to coast of Brazil and coasts of North America in early May and June. Present off Newfoundland Grand Banks all through northern summer. Many may move even further north then eastwards past Greenland into north-east Atlantic where they become abundant off south-west Ireland in September/October time. Infrequent round other parts of British coast. Most birds have left North Atlantic by November. In late autumn flocks of up to 200,000 birds are to be noted off Cape Cod, Massachusetts. This is believed to be a staging post in the movement of non-breeding birds.

Sooty Shearwater

Puffinus griseus 48cm (19in)

Nest	Twigs and dry leaves
Egg clutch	One
Egg colour	White
Laid	November
Incubation	Not known
Fledging	Not known

Identification A generally sooty brown bird, the overall dark plumage is relieved only by buffish or greyish white wing linings which can be variable in extent and many show as a wholly grey underwing.

The wings are long and narrow, set against a rather heavy-

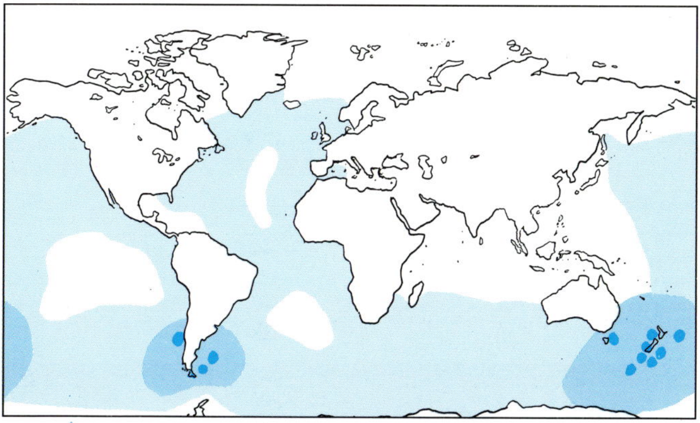

looking body. Flight is usually strong and direct comprising usually half a dozen quick stiff-winged flaps followed by a long glide. Careens in high winds. Plunge dives from about a metre above water. Attends trawlers but does not usually follow ships. Sexes alike, no seasonal variation.
Voice Generally silent at sea, but raucous calls and screams reported.
Habitat Nests on islands with rough tussocky grass, at other times mainly cold pelagic waters of southern hemisphere.
Food Mainly cephalopods, crustaceans and fish.
Range Breeds on islands off South America near Cape Horn, and perhaps islands of southern Chile. Also breeds in Australasia on islands off New South Wales, Tasmania, and especially off New Zealand at Snares, Auckland, Campbell, Chatham, Antipodes and Stewart Island, with some on islets in Foveaux Strait and Marquarie Island.
Movements A trans-equatorial migrant in Pacific and Atlantic Oceans. Returns to colonies September to November, with young birds leaving nest sites the following March to May. After breeding most South American birds depart north into Pacific. Some move north to Alaskan waters. Fewer birds observed along eastern US coast in early summer. From end of June, US east coast birds disperse eastwards across Atlantic and are then found in European waters mainly August to November, when not infrequently seen round British coasts, particularly east coast when sometimes noted in good numbers.

Birdwatchers in Britain eagerly search passing flocks of Manx Shearwaters to find a Sooty Shearwater, a scarce passage migrant, mainly noted along the south and east coast in autumn.

Manx Shearwater

Puffinus puffinus 30–38cm (12–15in)

Nest	Underground at end of metre-long tunnel excavated in soil
Egg clutch	One
Egg colour	White
Laid	End of May
Incubation	49–56 days
Fledging	46 days

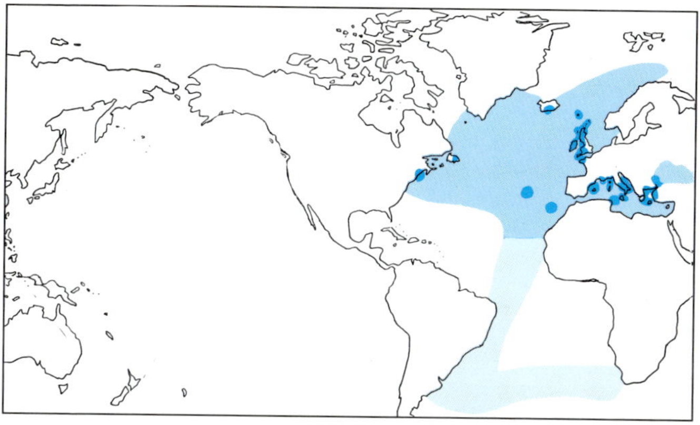

Identification Close views reveal a mainly black head to just below eye level with a slender bill hooked at the tip. As well as gleaming white underwing coverts, undertail coverts are also mostly white.

There are two subspecies. The East Mediterranean race, *P. p. yelkouan*, which is less sharply contrasting, while the West Mediterranean race, *P. p. mauretanicaus* (or Balearic race), is browner and even less contrasting than the nominate race. Flies in typical 'Shearwater' fashion with stiff outstretched, centrally placed wings presenting cross-like shape as it skims the waves, rising and falling as it does so. It has sharply contrasting black upperparts and white underparts. Also to be considered similar when trying to identify this species are Sooty Shearwater and Cory's Shearwater.

Voice When in nest-burrow utters various growls, croaks and cooing sounds. Silent at other times.

Habitat Favours turfy offshore islands for nesting. After breeding, lives at sea.

Food Small fish, cephalopods, small crustaceans and various surface foods.

Range In North Atlantic breeds Westmann Isles, Southern Iceland, Faeroes, Shetlands, Orkney and Inner Hebrides. Also Skokholm, Skomer, Anglesey and Isles of Scilly. Colonies on Blasketts off south-west Ireland; Puffin Island, County Kerry; smaller colonies off western and north-east Ireland. Some nest off Brittany coast, also Azores and Madeira.

Movements After nesting moves south to the main wintering areas of Atlantic waters off east coast of South America. When migrating, many can be seen around Britain, especially down west coast.

Storm Petrel

Hydrobates pelagicus 14–17cm ($5^1/_2$–$6^1/_2$in)

Nest	Often in a natural rock crevice or fissure, or under a boulder or rock, but will excavate own burrow in soft ground
Egg clutch	One
Egg colour	Dull white, with reddish spots at larger end
Laid	May
Incubation	38–43 days
Fledging	56–73 days

Identification Not unlike a large House-Martin, it flutters with bat-like flight interspersed with short glides just above the waves. The striking white rump contrasts with the rest of the plumage, which is dark, apart from a diagnostic white stripe on the underwing. At close range, a barely discernible pale diagonal bar can be seen on the upperwing. The black squarish tail helps to separate it from the similar Leach's Petrel. The smallest and darkest of the Atlantic Petrels, the legs are thin and black as is the slender, hook-tipped bill which has a long single tubular nostril above it. Frequently, storm-driven birds are often 'wrecked' well inland, especially in September and October.
Voice Musical creaking calls during night-time courtship chases. Also quiet murmuring sounds from incubating birds.
Habitat For nesting, rocky offshore islands. At other times, far out to sea.
Food Mainly zoo-plankton, small fish or small items of fish waste.
Range Breeds along the eastern coastline of the north Atlantic and the Western Mediterranean. The most northerly colony situated on Westmann Islands. Further south, found on Faeroes, Shetlands and Orkney. Certain parts of western coasts of Britain and Ireland. There are colonies breeding on islands off Sardinia, Sicily, the Balearics, Malta, and in the Adriatic.
Movements After nesting, birds head southwards to the sea around the Namibian and South African coast. The Mediterranean population remains in adjacent waters throughout the winter.

Frozen in the light of the photographer's flash, a Storm Petrel is seen flying to its nesting burrow under cover of darkness.

Leach's Petrel

Oceanodroma leucorhoa 45–48cm (18–19in)

Nest	Underground burrow excavated in soft peaty soil, usually lined with grass and bits of dry vegetation though sometimes no additional material at all. Also under boulders and in deserted stone buildings
Egg clutch	One
Egg colour	Dull white with reddish spots at the larger end
Laid	Beginning of June
Incubation	41–42 days
Fledging	63–70 days

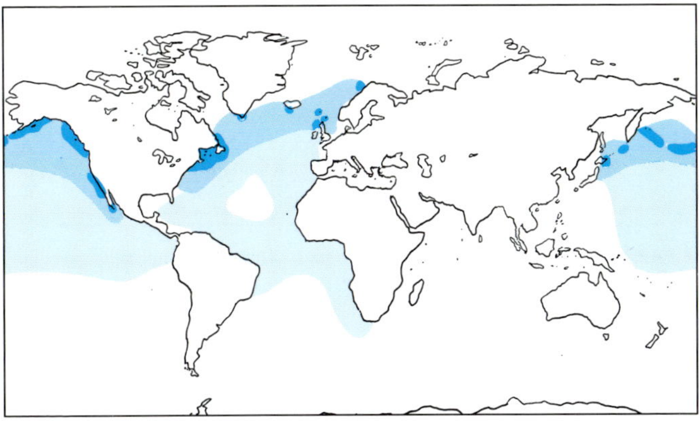

Identification Small seabird, only coming to land to breed or when storm-wrecked. Flies in a buoyant manner with a mixture of deep wing beats and shearwater-like glides. Blackish brown plumage with a pale diagonal bar along the upper wing. The amount of white on the rump varies but only at very close range can the dusky line dividing the rump be seen. Forked tail, (not square) is not always easy to detect. Unlike Wilson's Petrel (Appendix). It rarely patters feet across the sea when feeding, and does not follow ships.
Voice Crooning and chattering calls and at times high-pitched notes at breeding site.
Habitat Bleak, windswept islands for nesting; at other times the open sea.
Food Plankton, crustaceans, molluscs and small fish. Oily or fatty substances such as fish offal thrown from fishing vessels.
Range Breeds in huge numbers along the east coast of North America with major colonies at Nova Scotia, Massachusetts, Maine and Newfoundland. Small colonies nest in southern Greenland. In eastern Atlantic, breeds Faeroes, Lofoten Islands, also St Kilda group, Flannan, North Rona and Sula Sgeir.
Movements After nesting, generally disperses southwards. Atlantic-breeding birds believed to winter at the Gulf of Guinea and off Brazil. Around Britain, September gales make migrating birds more observable when blown closer to shore. At times some are blown inland and are seen at large reservoirs.

A truly pelagic species, Leach's Petrels are usually only to be seen well away from the shore but severe weather can drive them landwards.

Gannet

Sula bassana 87–100cm (34–39in)

Nest A pile of seaweed and grass plus some feathers. Can be 30–60cm (1–2ft) high, though sometimes just a depression in the ground
Egg clutch One or two
Egg colour On laying, a pale translucent blue turning white, becoming stained yellow and brown
Laid April to May
Incubation 44 days
Fledging 90 days

Identification A large, dazzlingly white bird with long narrow wings tipped with black, spanning 2m (6ft). In flight, distinctive cigar-shaped body and large size should help identify the species. In breeding plumage head and neck are tinged yellowish buff.

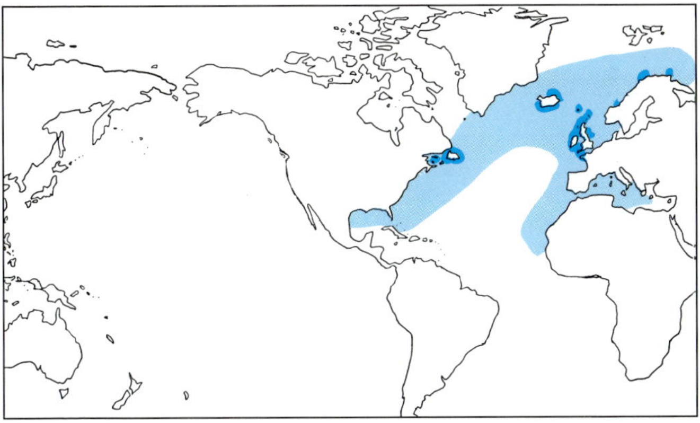

The spear-shaped bill is slate blue with a horn-coloured tip. The legs are slate blue with toes and tarsus lined with green. A newly hatched bird is black and featherless. Develops downy-white plumage, later turns dark speckled white by the time it leaves the nest. Over next three years immature birds become progressively whiter starting from the head, rump and underparts. Gannets plunge dive for food, often from heights of 10m (32ft), creating a spectacular sight, especially when many birds, attracted by a shoal of fish, hit the water one after another.
Voice Silent except at nest site where it makes loud croaking sounds.
Habitat Breeds cliffs and tops of rock islands. In winter disperses mainly to continental shelf water and adjacent seas.
Food Turns underwater to take fish such as cod, pollack, whiting, haddock, sprats, pilchards, mackerel and eels.
Range Most breeding colonies located in eastern Atlantic mainly Britain, but some Ireland, Iceland, Faeroes, Norway and one in France. Remainder are to be found on the Canadian eastern seaboard in the Gulf of St Lawrence.
Movements After nesting, most British birds move south to winter in sub-tropical waters and even tropical waters off West Africa. Some stay in region of the North Sea and Bay of Biscay area.

The adult Gannet in its all-white plumage with black-tipped wings, is surely one of the world's most impressive seabirds.

Cormorant

Phalacrocorax carbo 80–101cm (30½–40in)

Nest	A large heap of rotting seaweed
Egg clutch	Three to four
Egg colour	Pale blue covered with a chalky deposit
Laid	April to May
Incubation	28 days
Fledging	84 days

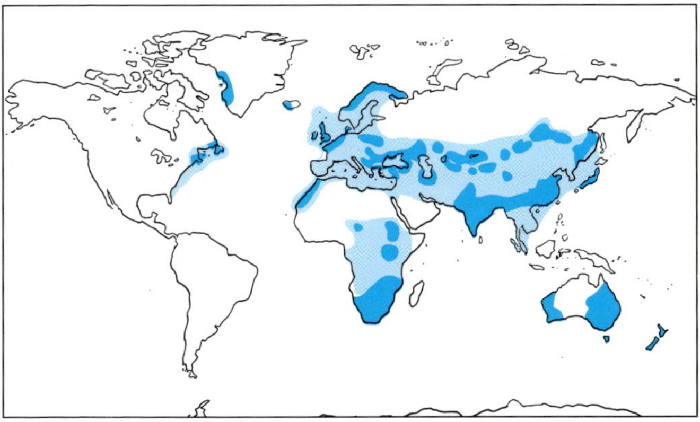

Identification Basically a dark, long-necked bird, which frequently perches on rocks, buoys, or posts where it will stand in heraldic pose drying its wings. In breeding plumage, the bronze-brown or black feathering on the upperparts is contrasted by a white cheek and white thigh patch which distinguishes it from other cormorants. The bill is stout with yellow gular area. Non-breeding plumage is similar but lacks white thigh patch. Flies low over the water with strong regular beats of its wings, and neck outstretched. When in a group, they fly line astern reminiscent of geese. On water, swims with neck and back awash, with head inclined upwards. In this pose could be mistaken for a diver (*Gavia* sp.). A lively bird, constantly looking this way and that, it frequently dives when feeding and invariably brings the catch to the surface before swallowing it.
Voice Loud guttural croakings at the nest.
Habitat Rocky coasts favoured for nesting with a preference for cliff ledges and rocky islets. Tree nest sites and reed beds are used at inland locations.
Food Fish of all sorts but especially herring.
Range In the North Atlantic, breeds southern Greenland, Iceland, Britain, Ireland and along other suitable north European coastal areas; breeds at some inland sites in Holland, Germany, Austria, Czechoslovakia, Hungary, Rumania.
Movements British and Irish populations are non-migratory, but disperse widely throughout adjacent waters, usually within 50 miles of the coast. Some move inland to large reservoirs.

The Cormorant is a common sight around Britain's coast. It is increasingly noted at inland locations during winter months.

Double-crested Cormorant

Phalacrocorax auritus 74–91cm (29–36in)

Nest	A bulky structure of sticks and seaweed
Egg clutch	Three to four
Egg colour	Pale greenish-blue with chalky deposit
Laid	April to July
Incubation	28 days
Fledging	60 days

Identification In breeding plumage appears basically black with a green gloss to the head and body. At close range in good light the mantle and wing coverts are seen to be deep bronzy-brown with blackish borders to the feathers forming a neat scaled

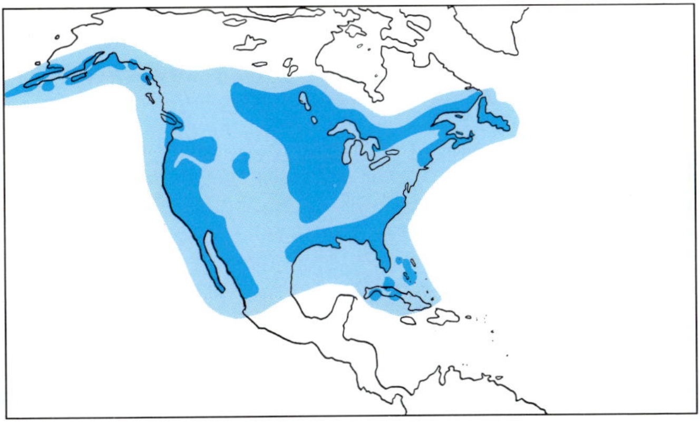

pattern. The eye is green, the bill greyish horn and the facial skin and gular pouch are a conspicuous orange-yellow. Despite its name, the crest is not obvious. Non-breeding plumage is basically similar though less glossy green. The juvenile is dull brown or brownish black with a scaled appearance to mantle and coverts. The head is similar with a paler, slightly mottled, throat and breast. The bill is pink or yellow with a darker culmen. The facial skin and gular pouch are yellowish. This is the only species of cormorant likely to be seen in the interior of North America or in freshwater habitats. On the Atlantic coast compare with Great Cormorant.

Voice During courtship gives a series of 'oak-oak-oak' and a loud 'r-r-r-o-o-o-o-p' as well as a variety of croaks and squeaks. Silent at other times.

Habitat Nests on rocky coasts or cliffs and islands. Also breeds in trees by inland waters.

Food Almost entirely fish.

Range Most common and widespread North American Cormorant breeding all around the coast from southern Alaska and Aleutian Islands south to the Gulf of California, the Gulf coast, and in the east found as far north as Newfoundland. Also in the interior as far north as Alberta. Also found in Cuba, the Bahamas and Isle of Pines.

Movements Northern and inland populations move south to winter south in Honduras and the Caribbean. A Double-crested Cormorant seen at Charlton Pond, Billingham, Cleveland in January 1989 is the first for Britain and a first for the Western Palearctic if accepted by the British Ornithologists' Union.

A Double-crested Cormorant hangs its wings out to dry in typical heraldic pose.

Shag

Phalacrocorax aristotelis 76cm (30in)

Nest	A flattish heap of vegetation which can include bracken or heather for a base, but normally consists mostly of seaweed
Egg clutch	Three, occasionally up to six
Egg colour	Pale blue with a chalky deposit
Laid	March to late April
Incubation	30–31 days
Fledging	53 days

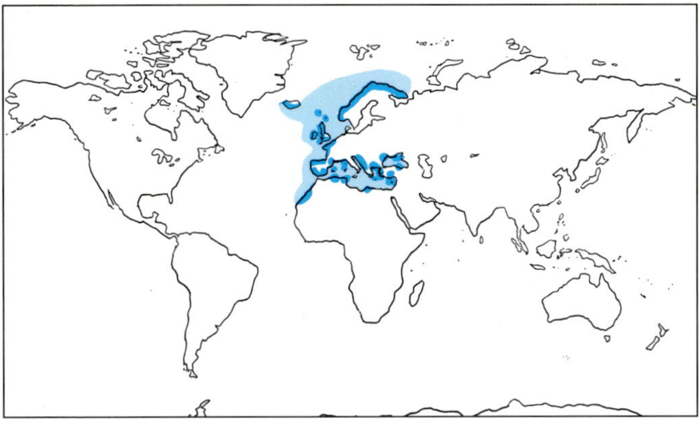

Identification Slightly smaller than Cormorant. In breeding plumage, sports a distinctive upcurved crest while the dark plumage will be seen to have a greenish gloss which gives rise to its alternative name of Green Cormorant. At close quarters it will be noted that the black gular pouch is spotted with yellow, with the skin at the base of the slender-hooked bill a chrome-yellow. The large, webbed feet are black. The eye is emerald green. Immature birds are dark brown showing little or no white in the breast. Perches in heraldic pose in order to dry wings but is less inclined to perch on buoys or posts than the Cormorant. Takes flight from water with some difficulty, splashing along with its wings and threshing the water with its feet for some distance before becoming airborne. Flight is steady and close to the water's surface.
Voice Various guttural croaks when at nest, otherwise silent.
Habitat Nests on rocky cliffs and islands, often favouring concealed sites inside caves. Prefers a more marine environment than the Cormorant and is less frequent around sandy estuaries.
Food Mainly sprats and sand eels.
Range Breeds western Iceland, the Faeroes, Britain, Ireland, the Channel Islands and from the Kola peninsula in the USSR to Stavanger, Norway, with some nesting at sites off the coast of Brittany, France and Spain. There are two subspecies: *P. a. riggenbachi* breeding in North Africa and *P. a. demarestii* breeding in the Mediterranean basin, from the Balearics eastwards to the Crimea.
Movements After nesting, the birds move to the open sea, with the young tending to spread farther afield – some British-bred birds reach waters off the coast of Spain and into the Mediterranean.

Pygmy Cormorant

Phalacrocorax pygmeus 45–55cm (18–21½in)

Nest	An untidy, relatively flimsy structure of twigs or reeds, in trees or in thick reed beds. Bird's droppings quickly bind the nest material together
Egg clutch	Four to six
Egg colour	Pale green, covered with a chalky deposit
Laid	May, early June
Incubation	27–30 days
Fledging	Around 70 days

Identification A small, short-necked, round-headed, long-tailed cormorant, much more active than its larger brethren, it recalls a coot (*Fulica atra*) when in flight.

In breeding plumage both sexes have a dark brown head and glossy greenish-black plumage spotted with white. The scapulars and wing coverts are grey with black edgings. There is a slight crest.

The bill and the featherless area around the eyes and the legs and feet are dark brownish black. The female is slightly smaller and less well marked and coloured than the male. After breeding the white feathers are lost, the throat becomes white and the breast red brown. Immature birds have blackish grey upperparts with whitish grey underparts, becoming almost pure white on the throat and belly. The flanks and undertail coverts are black and the bill yellow.

Voice Utters various croaking calls during breeding season, otherwise apparently silent.

Habitat During breeding season, favours freshwater lakes with reedbeds, also swamps and other well vegetated wetlands where fish abound. In winter resorts more often to brackish or salt water.

Food Mainly fish, but also shrimps and other crustaceans as available.

Range Breeds Yugoslavia, Rumania, Greece, Turkey, Crimea, Iran, Caspian and Aral Seas. Has occurred as vagrant in Sweden, France, Tunisia and Pakistan.

Movements Returns to colonies March/April. After breeding disperses generally southwards but not to great distances from the breeding areas, where some remain throughout year. Population generally in decline.

The population of the Pygmy Cormorant is declining and is further threatened by the destruction of its wetland habitat.

American White Pelican

Pelecanus erythrorhynchos 127–178cm (50–70in)

Nest	Shallow depression lined with small sticks, some grass and sometimes one or two feathers
Egg clutch	Two to three
Egg colour	White
Laid	April to June
Incubation	28 days
Fledging	62 days

Identification In breeding plumage an all-white bird with a small pale yellow crest and a bright orange bill; this usually has a fibrous plate on the upper mandible, which is shed during the nesting period. The eye is orange-yellow with an orange orbital ring, while the face skin is yellow and the legs and large, webbed

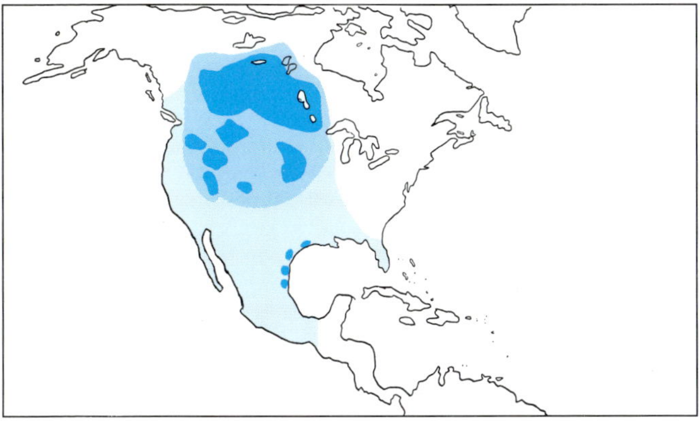

feet are orange-red. Flies with neck hunched back to the body and slow deliberate flaps of the wings followed by long glides. It is then that the distinctive black primaries and secondaries can be seen. Be careful not to mistake for Wood Stork, Whooping Crane or Snow Goose, which show similar black and white plumage in flight. A good distinction however is that these three species fly with their necks outstretched. The immature looks like the parent but the gular pouch and facial skin is grey while the crown, nape and hind neck are brownish. The primaries and secondaries are also brown. May be up to four years before attains adult plumage.

Voice Nasal grunting at nest site, otherwise generally silent.

Habitat Prefers freshwater, nesting in colonies mainly on islands of inland lakes.

Food Almost entirely fish, obtained by scooping up prey with huge bill. Often feeds in groups, threshing water with wings to herd fish into suitable shallow water.

Range Breeds mainly in North American provinces with scattered breeding centres in east Washington State, south and north California, west Nevada, south Idaho, north Utah, Montana, Wyoming and the Dakotas, Minnesota and coastal Texas.

Movements After nesting, birds gather in large flocks, particularly in area of the southern Great Plains, and move to wintering grounds in the Gulf of Mexico, Florida, and the coasts of Central America south to the West Indies and Guatemala. In western USA winters along coast of central California southward to Gulf of California with stragglers reaching eastern Alaska. Scarce north to Nova Scotia, on the eastern North American coast.

Brown Pelican

Pelecanus occidentalis 114cm (45in)

Nest	A colonial nester, it builds a bulky structure of twigs in a variety of nest sites, including trees, bushes, mangroves. At times on the ground, when little material is employed
Egg clutch	Two to four, sometimes up to six
Egg colour	White
Laid	May
Incubation	28 days
Fledging	35–70 days

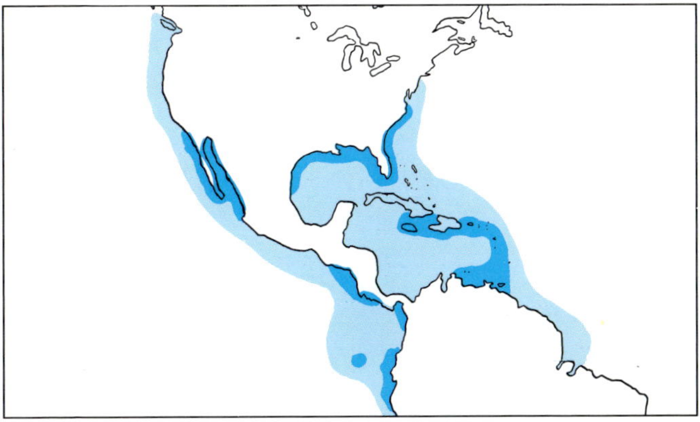

Identification At a distance in breeding plumage, it looks a darkish bird, but a close view reveals that forehead, crown and ear coverts are white with a tinge of yellow. The upperparts are silver-grey but have a warm, brownish look. The underparts are blackish brown. The eye is pale yellow with a pink orbital ring, blue-grey facial skin and blue-grey to black legs and feet. Flies powerfully with slow methodical flaps of huge wings.
Voice Generally silent.
Habitat Entirely coastal and rarely seen any distance away from the sea.
Food Mainly fish caught by diving into sea from 10m (30ft) or more above the waves.
Range Confined to North and South America. There are six subspecies. The nominate race breeds in the West Indies. *P. o. carolinensis* breeds along the coasts of tropical America from Southern Carolina south to the Orinoco, while on the Pacific coast *P. o. californicus* is found from California south to Mexico.
Movements Partial migrants in their more northerly range, movements are erratic and depend very much on local conditions as to whether they stay or leave.

An adult Brown Pelican ruffles its feathers as it preens, creating a most unusual plumage pattern.

Pomarine Skua

Stercorarius pomarinus 65–78cm ($25^1/_2$–31in)

Nest	Shallow depression with a minimal lining of finer vegetation
Egg clutch	Two
Egg colour	Brown, blotched olive
Laid	June
Incubation	26 days
Fledging	30 days

Identification Skuas look like dark gulls but are distinguished by elongated tail feathers, slender wings more angled at carpel joint and have aggressive, piratical feeding habits.

In breeding plumage, Pomarine Skua adults are readily identified by their central tail feathers which extend well beyond rest of tail and are twisted into a spoon shape at the tip. Slightly smaller than the Great Skua, it is always larger and more heavily built than the Arctic Skua, and its deep-chested, broad-winged appearance gives a greater impression of power.

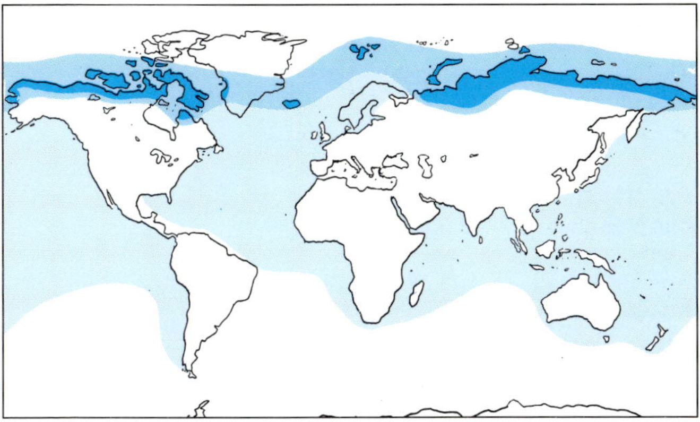

There are two colour phases: light phase birds usually show a dark brown crown and whitish underparts which are often crossed by a broad dark brown breast band. The ventral area is also usually dark and there is often a yellowish tinge to the sides of the neck. The upperparts are generally plain dark brown with a white flash at the base of the primaries. Dark phase birds are blackish brown with a darker crown, the white wing flashes contrasting strongly with the rest of the upperwing in flight. The dark colour phase usually comprises less than 20 per cent of any population. Young birds and non-breeding adults are more difficult to identify and are best separated from Arctic Skua by larger size and heavier build.

Voice Various low-pitched 'gack' or 'geek' calls and other gull-like cries.

Habitat When breeding, at tundra near coast but also near lakes and rivers. At other times far out to sea.

Food When breeding, mainly lemmings but also birds. At other times mostly fish, either obtained by forcing other birds to disgorge, or by catching own prey.

Range Breeding range is circumpolar nesting in Alaska, north central Canada, Greenland to Spitsbergen in Norway and across Siberia. Winters in Atlantic off coast of West Africa and around Caribbean. Some birds visit the Indian Ocean, whilst in Pacific, many winter as far south as south-east Australia and off coasts of South America.

Movements After nesting, adults move southwards from end of August, with juveniles following late September and October. A relatively scarce passage migrant to Britain, following migrating shearwaters and terns, when can be seen moving along English Channel and off the Scottish coast mainly in August and September.

Arctic Skua

Stercorarius parasiticus 46–67cm (18–26½in)

Nest A depression on a dry patch amongst more marshy ground
Egg clutch Two
Egg colour Dark, blotched above
Laid May to June
Incubation 21–28 days
Fledging 28–35 days

Identification As Pomarine Skua, has two distinct colour phases, as well as a puzzling range of intermediates. The dark phase is predominant in the south of the breeding range with a greater proportion of pale phase birds occurring in the north. About the size of a Common Gull, adults are dark blackish brown above with a small white flash at the base of the outer primaries. Pale phase birds are creamy white below with a dark brown

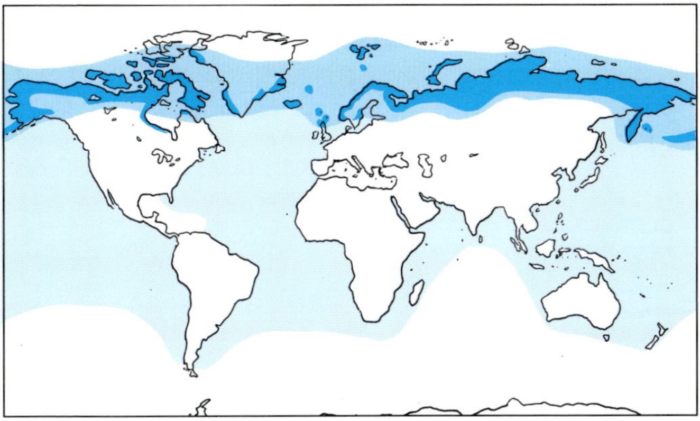

underwing ventral area and undertail. Also shows a contrasting black crown separated by a pale nape, while the side of the neck shows a yellowish wash and on some birds there may be a darker breast band. The dark phase is essentially dark blackish brown all over. All adults have long pointed extensions to their two central tail feathers, but never as long as Long-tailed Skua. Unless twisted tail feathers of Pomarine can be seen, best distinguished from that species by smaller size and lighter build. Juveniles are mainly dark above with many showing pale underparts. Young birds generally show only a short extension to their two central tail feathers.

The distinctive Skua behaviour of chasing other birds to make them disgorge their food is typical of the species.

Voice Hoarse Kittiwake-like calls and various buzzard-like mews at nest site.

Habitat Grassy or mossy tundra with ponds or lake when breeding. At other times over the sea.

Food During breeding season will take small birds, their eggs, mammals and at times insects and berries. Otherwise much of food is obtained by harrying other birds to make them disgorge or drop food they have caught.

Range Widely distributed, breeding around the entire high Arctic from Alaska across the northern Canadian coast through Greenland, Iceland, Orkney, Shetlands and certain scattered Scottish mainland localities, Scandinavia and extending right across northern Siberia.

Movements A leisurely southwards migration commences from early August well into October, moving singly or in small groups. In Britain quite frequently noted inland at migration times. It is believed the majority of Atlantic birds will cross the Equator where they winter off Argentina and Southern Africa.

Long-tailed Skua

Stercorarius longicaudus 50–58cm (19½–23in)

Nest	A shallow depression on open ground usually a dry spot such as slightly raised hummock. Small pieces of lichen often added during incubation
Egg clutch	Two, occasionally three
Egg colour	Glossy olive-green to brown with dark brown, grey spots at front end
Laid	June to July
Incubation	23 days
Fledging	21 days

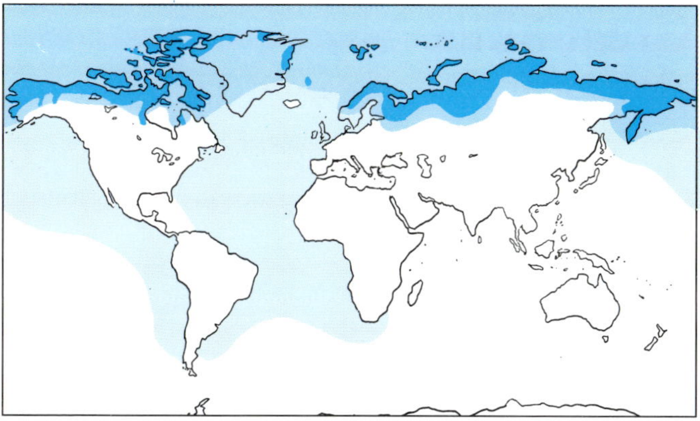

Identification Smallest of the Skuas, the long central tail feathers extending 12–25cm (5–10in) beyond the rest of the tail make it the same length as the other bulkier skuas. Presents a much 'cleaner' appearance than either Arctic or Pomarine Skuas, showing completely whitish underparts with no sign of a breast band. Also shows a more clear-cut black cap which contrasts with a broad white collar and a pale back, while the cheeks are a clean yellow. The bill is black and the legs grey. The flight is light and airy with shallow wing beats and it shows less white in the wing than either Arctic or Pomarine Skuas. The immature bird, though often indistinguishable from the young Arctic Skua, is greyer and has little or no white in the wing. At close range it usually shows a pale hind collar and bolder barring on the tail coverts.
Voice Generally silent but utters various shrill cries when on breeding grounds.
Habitat Flat coastal tundra, stony plateaux or vegetated upland when breeding. At other times far out to sea.
Food At breeding site, mammals especially lemmings, also insects, berries, also eggs of other birds. At other times will catch fish, but more often than not steals from other birds in typical piratical Skua behaviour.
Range Breeds in both high and low Arctic nesting on islands and along coasts of the Arctic Ocean, south to the tundra region of North America and Eurasia.
Movements Leaves breeding grounds from late August and moves southwards overland, continuing on out to sea with widespread dispersal to Atlantic and Pacific Oceans.

An adult Long-tailed Skua shows its long, wispy tail streamers.

Great Skua

Stercorarius skua 53–58cm (21–23in)

Nest	A scrape often with a lining of grassy materials
Egg clutch	Two
Egg colour	Light stone to reddish brown with dark spots and blotches
Laid	May to June
Incubation	23–30 days
Fledging	42 days

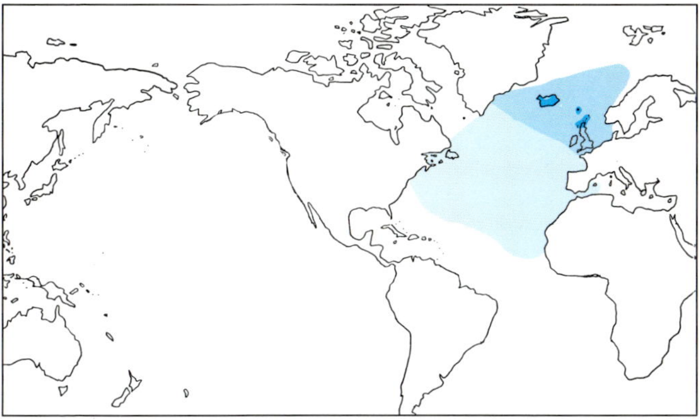

Identification About the size of a Herring Gull, it is larger and bulkier than other Skuas of North Atlantic waters. The plumage is fairly uniform dark brown. At close quarters however, pale streakings are visible on the neck and upperparts. The wings are broad and quite rounded which separates it from other slender-winged Skuas. The piratical behaviour of this and other Skuas is generally sufficient to identify the Family for they relentlessly chase terns, gulls and at times even Gannets.

When in flight, the dark overall appearance of the Great Skua might render it unidentifiable at a distance were it not for the prominent white wing patches formed by the white base of the primaries, which signal its presence even when far out at sea.

Voice Generally silent, but utters a repeated 'ek-ek-ek-ek' call during display at nest site.

Habitat For nesting, grassy areas or heather moorland near to sea. At other times out to sea.

Food Mainly fish – caught, scavenged or pirated from other birds. Will also kill and eat other birds.

Range Confined while breeding to the North Atlantic, nesting in Iceland, Faeroes, Shetland, Orkney and northern Scotland. Recently recorded breeding in Spitsbergen and Finnmark.

Movements After nesting, leaves breeding area and becomes totally pelagic, wandering the North Atlantic.

In flight the Great Skua, or Bonxie as it is often called, can be identified at long distance by its prominent white wing patches.

Mediterranean Gull

Larus melanocephalus 38–43cm (15–17in)

Nest	A shallow scrape in bare sandy ground or in low vegetation
Egg clutch	Three
Egg colour	Creamy to buff, speckled with dark brown
Laid	Mid-May to end of June
Incubation	23–25 days
Fledging	35–40 days

Identification In breeding plumage, the hood is black with a conspicuous broken white eye ring; the upperparts are pale grey, (paler than Black-headed Gull) and the wing tips are white. The bill and legs are bright red. The non-breeding adult has a white head with a variable dark shadow behind the eye. The white wing

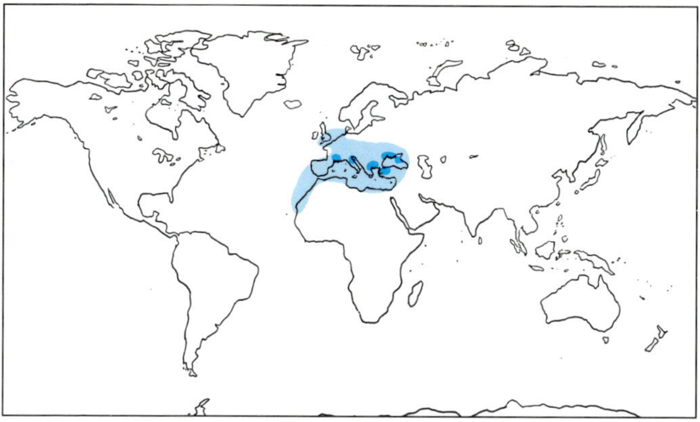

tips are an excellent distinction between this species and Black-headed Gull whether perched or flying. In immature plumage, identification is more of a problem. First-winter birds have a pale grey mantle, blackish outer primaries and secondaries, and a black tail band. Its greater bulk, heavier-looking bill, blacker primary tips and head markings should help differentiate from first-winter Black-headed Gull. In flight, recalls a young Common Gull, differing from that species in the greater contrast between its blacker outer primaries and secondaries, and the pale mid-wing panel and pale grey mantle. The head, body and underparts are also much whiter than any first-winter Common Gull.

Voice On nesting grounds, gives long 'whaa-whaa-whaa-whaa-whaa--oo-ah' call, much like a Lesser Black-backed Gull. In flight sometimes utters a tern-like 'kee-er' note.

Habitat Lowland areas of deltas, estuaries, lagoons, marshes and inland waters when breeding, at other times coastal locations.

Food Small fish and other marine life, also earthworms and a variety of insects at times.

Range Breeds mainly Black Sea coast of USSR with some on Mediterranean shores of Greece, Italy and France. Has attempted to breed in Britain.

Movements After breeding, birds disperse in all directions to mainly winter on Atlantic coast of Morocco, Portugal and Spain. Increasing numbers winter along coasts of English Channel and North Sea. Vagrants have been noted in Sweden, Norway, Kuwait and Kenya.

In summer plumage the Mediterranean Gull, with its broken white eye ring, scarlet bill with yellow tip and scarlet legs, is easy to identify.

Laughing Gull

Larus atricilla 38–43cm (15–17in)

Nest	Constructed of grass, weeds and other vegetation on ground, usually in sandy areas with plenty of low vegetation
Egg clutch	Three
Egg colour	Buffy to olive, spotted with brown over grey or purple
Laid	April to July
Incubation	20–23 days
Fledging	24 days

Identification The adult is dark grey above, about the same shade as a Franklin's Gull, and has the same neat contrasting white trailing edge to the wing. The wing tips, however, are solidly black and unlike the Franklin's Gull the tail is all-white. In breeding plumage there is a black hood with a broken white

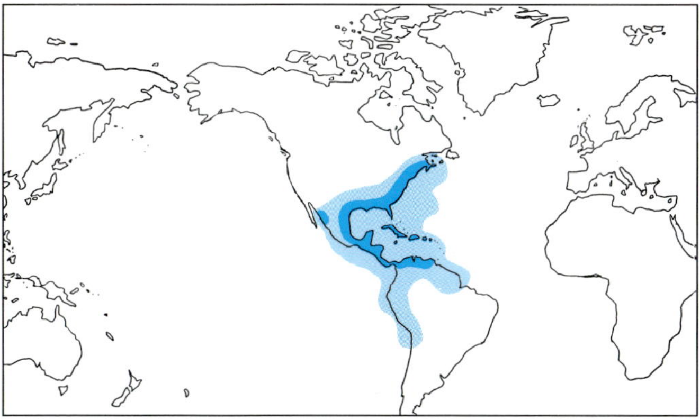

eye-ring. The bill and legs are dull red. Although the size of a Common Gull, the legs are longer and more slender, and together with its more pointed wings it has a more rakish appearance both on the ground and in the air than either the Common or Franklin's Gulls. It is characterized at all ages by the heavy dark 'drooping bill' which, together with a long sloping forehead, gives its head a rather 'snout-like' profile. In winter the head is white with a variably streaked greyish-brown wash on the ear coverts and rear crown. The bill and legs are then blackish. The juvenile is a very dark bird with mantle and wing coverts greyish brown with neat pale fringes that give a scalloped pattern. Bill and legs are blackish.

Voice A strident laughing 'ha-ha-ha' from which the bird gets its name.

Habitat Mainly coastal bays and estuaries. Though generally found on rivers only in tidal reaches, will often visit fresh water near coast. Otherwise rare inland, except at the Great Lakes, USA, where fairly regular.

Food Small fish. Sometimes takes eggs. Scavenges like other gulls, and will follow the plough to feed on earthworms.

Range Breeds east coast of North America from Nova Scotia south to Florida, around the Gulf of Mexico, on Caribbean islands and south to Venezuela. On Pacific Coast breeds in Mexico from Sinora to Sinola. Winters from North Carolina south along the coasts of South America to northern Brazil and Northern Chile occasionally as far north as California. In Britain there were only two records before 1958. Since then around 50 sightings have been made in all months of the year except March.

Movements Northern populations move south after breeding.

An adult Laughing Gull in full breeding plumage.

Franklin's Gull

Larus pipixcan 33–38cm (13–15in)

Nest	Scraps of vegetation form floating platform anchored to the bottom of shallow water
Egg clutch	Three
Egg colour	Buff-brown or greenish-buff spotted and blotched brown
Laid	May to June
Incubation	24 days
Fledging	35 days

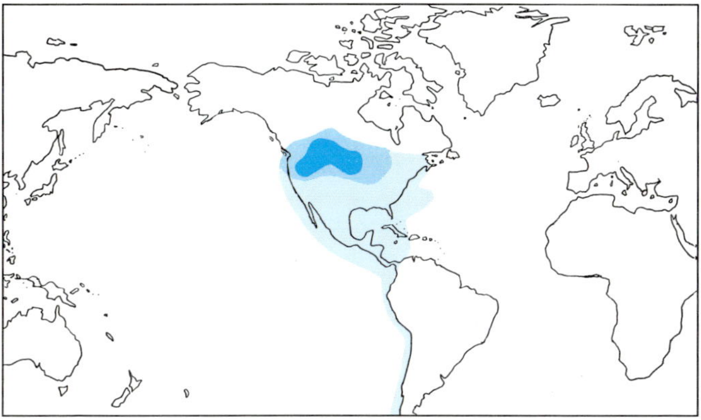

Identification Distinctly smaller than Laughing Gull, it is much more compact with a higher, more rounded crown, relatively shorter bill and legs, and broader more paddle-shaped wings. In adult plumage, the upperparts are mud to dark grey, neatly set-off by a white trailing edge to the wing. The outer primaries are tipped white, backed by a blackish band and then show a further narrow white band which separates the tips from the wings. This pattern immediately distinguishes it from Laughing Gull. Another diagnostic feature is the pale grey centre of the tail but this is usually difficult to see. In breeding plumage the hood is black with a broken white eye-ring; the bill is red with a narrow black subterminal band; the feet are red and the underparts may show a delicate rosy flush. In winter it has a blackish half-hood on the back of the head while the bill and legs fade to dull red or blackish. Juveniles are brown scaled with white above. Primaries are blackish and there is a white trailing edge to the wing. The forehead and underparts are whitish and the tail shows a black terminal band. Bill and legs are blackish.
Voice Generally silent, breeding birds may give a soft 'krruk'.
Habitat In USA frequents prairie sloughs, lakes and marshes when breeding. At other times coastal locations.
Food Hawks for insects or dips in water to take morsels of food from surface.
Range Breeds northern Alberta, south to north-west Utah and north-west Iowa. Winters mainly from Guatemala southwards.
Movements After breeding moves south across the Great Plain and the Rockies and down west coast Americas as far south as the Strait of Magellan at the tip of Chile. Not recorded in Britain before 1970. Since then there have been about a dozen records of birds which have crossed the Atlantic.

Little Gull

Larus minutus 25–30cm (10–12in)

Nest Sometimes just a scrape, but at times a more substantial semi-floating structure
Egg clutch Two or three
Egg colour Olive-green with blotches of grey, brown or black
Laid May to June
Incubation 23–25 days
Fledging 21–24 days

Identification The world's smallest gull, which can often be distinguished by size alone. However at all seasons it is the dark underwing that quickly identifies the adult; even at long distances over the sea note that the wing tips have a slightly rounded look and the tail is square-ended. In breeding plumage the Little Gull has a more complete and darker black head than either a Black-headed Gull or Bonaparte's Gull. In non-breeding

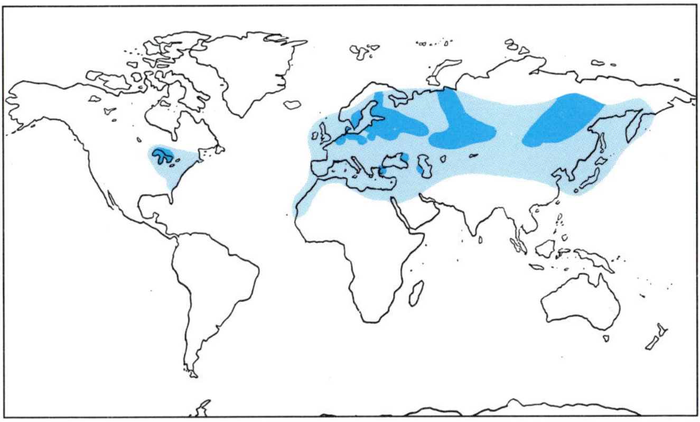

plumage the white head has a dusky-grey crown and black ear spot. The underparts are white and when in full breeding condition, show a suffusion of pink on the breast, while the back and upperwing are pale blue-grey. The short legs are red and the small pointed bill is reddish brown.

The juvenile is quite distinctive and in its first year plumage shows black outer primaries which contrast sharply with the grey white-tipped inner primaries. This pattern of black continues from the carpal joint across the secondary coverts to form an 'M' pattern along the whole of the wing. The juvenile Kittiwake shows a similar pattern but is larger and has a black collar which Little Gull does not have.

Voice During display flights calls with a shrill, rapid rhythmic 'ke-ko, ke-ko'. At other times silent.

Habitat Mainly breeds by lakes or on freshwater wetlands of river basins, though some nest on coast.

Food At sea mainly small fish, but in other situations a wide range of invertebrates are taken. A large number of insects such as dragonflies, mayflies and stoneflies are also caught.

Range Breeds mainly in eastern and western Siberia, also locally in the Baltic basin and in isolated colonies in the Netherlands, Denmark and Sweden. They also nest in south-east Europe, mainly Poland and the Black Sea area. Has attempted to nest in Britain on a few occasions.

Movements Adults and juveniles leave their nesting grounds towards the end of July, but the family groups soon split up to disperse throughout the main wintering areas of the Black Sea, the Mediterranean and beyond. Many reach the North Sea via the Baltic, and off the Dutch coast large numbers can be seen in the autumn. Often quite numerous in British waters and occasionally inland.

Sabine's Gull

Larus sabini 33–36cm (13–14in)

Nest	A shallow scrape, sparsely lined, though at times a more substantial cup of moss, seaweed and feathers
Egg clutch	Two to three
Egg colour	Olive to buff-olive
Laid	June
Incubation	23–25 days
Fledging	20–25 days

Identification A most handsome bird in its breeding plumage, with a grey head separated from the white neck and body by a narrow black collar. The upperparts are bluish grey and when at rest the black primaries show prominent white patches. The bill is black with a yellow tip, and although difficult to see, the gape is red. The legs are black. In flight this bird shows a most

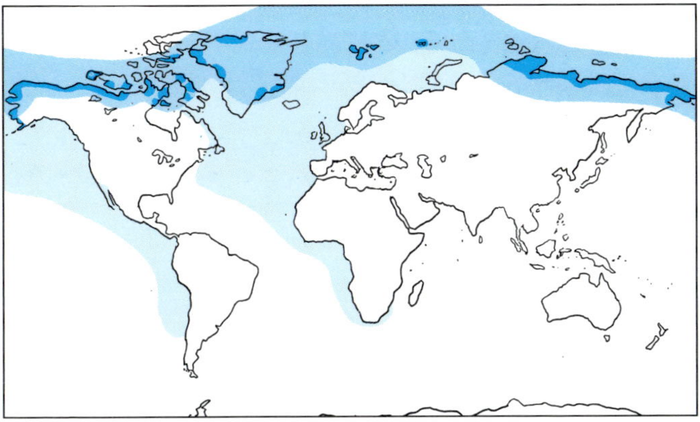

distinctive field mark; a striking arrangement of black, grey and white triangles in the wing. Grey in the middle, (greyish brown in immature birds) with black on the outer primaries and white on the secondaries and inner primaries. The tail is slightly forked and a black subterminal is found in the immature bird. In autumn the head is mostly white with a dark grey necklace on the nape while the legs are flesh-grey. First-winter birds have brown head and body, black bills and pinkish legs. The distinctive wing pattern identifies the Sabine's Gull at all ages.
Voice Hard grating calls (not dissimilar to Arctic Tern). Most vociferous on breeding grounds.
Habitat When breeding, favours marshy flat tundra and low-lying areas with shallow brackish pools, especially those containing islets or narrow peninsulas. At other times, pelagic.
Food Small fish, insects, crustaceans. Will take eggs of other birds.
Range A circumpolar breeding species: nests west Alaska, Greenland, the Canadian Arctic and western Siberia. Has bred Spitsbergen.
Movements After breeding, the birds gather along the coast line before moving south. Those from Siberia together with most of Alaskan population move south-east across the Pacific en route to South American coast of Columbia and Peru, occasionally reaching northern Chile.

The Canadian and Greenland population move across the Atlantic to north-western European waters when considerable numbers have also been reported off Cape Finnistere (Ireland). In recent years has been more frequently recorded in British waters on both east and west coasts, and especially St Ives Bay, Cornwall. Birds then continue on to Namibia and the South African coast.

Bonaparte's Gull

Larus philadelphia 33–36cm (13–14in)

Nest	Composed of twigs, grass moss and lichen, it is usually placed in a spruce tree, rarely on the ground
Egg clutch	Three
Egg colour	Buffy-grey or buffy-green, blotched with brown
Laid	June to July
Incubation	24 days
Fledging	35–42 days

Identification In breeding plumage it has a slate-black hood with white crescents above and below the eye. The bill is black with a reddish base. The upperparts are dark grey and for a brief period there is a rosy flush to the white underparts. In non-breeding plumage it loses the black hood, having instead just two small blackish spots – one just in front of the eye, the other on the ear coverts. The upperwing is grey with white forewing and blackish

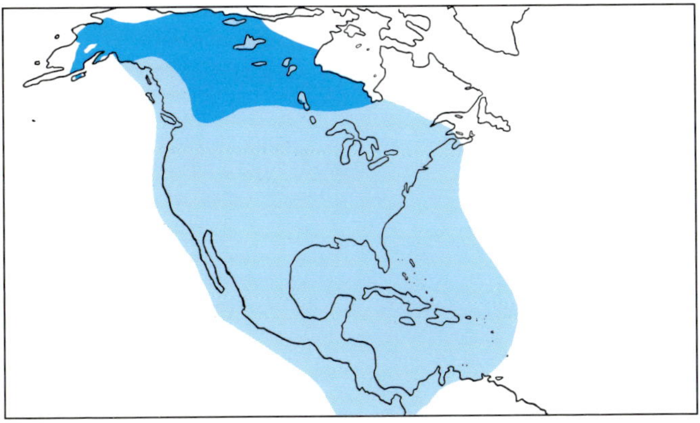

tips to outer primaries. Underwing coverts grey and outer primaries white with black tips. Compare Black-headed, which has dusky outer primaries. As well as a blackish crown, the juvenile has a white head with two blackish spots like a non-breeding adult. It has brown upperparts mottled with buff and a white rump and white tail with a blackish terminal band. The wing coverts are a mixture of pale grey and blackish feathers, the darker feathers forming a carpal bar across the wing. The flight feathers are pale grey-white with a black edge to the primaries and secondaries as well as blackish outer primaries. The bill is black and the legs flesh coloured. The first-winter bird is similar, but the brown of the mantle is replaced by pale grey and the black crown is lost.

Voice A distinctive chattering call, a coot-like cackling.

Habitat Favours the muskeg – open coniferous woodland near ponds and lakes in lowland areas when breeding. Outside nesting season haunts bays, harbours, sand and mudflats. Also occurs inland on rivers and marshes, especially around the Great Lakes.

Food Crustaceans and insects picked from surface of water either in flight or when swimming.

Range Breeds Alaska and Canada extending from northern Manitoba south to southern British Columbia and Central Ontario. Winters along the American west coast from Washington south to Sinola in Mexico. Also found from the Great Lakes south along the major rivers – especially the Mississippi to the Gulf Coast and the Caribbean. On east coast found from Massachusetts southwards. Some of these birds have drifted across the Atlantic and since 1958 there have been around 50 records of Bonaparte's Gull in Britain.

Movements In North America, after nesting, birds form into large flocks often comprising thousands of birds.

Black-headed Gull

Larus ridibundus 38–43cm (15–17in)

Nest	Varies from a sizeable construction of reed and grasses in west situations to just a few strands of grass, straw or other handy materials in flat drier settings
Egg clutch	Two or three
Egg colour	Pale blue to green to deep brown, blotched dark brown
Laid	April
Incubation	22–24 days
Fledging	35–42 days

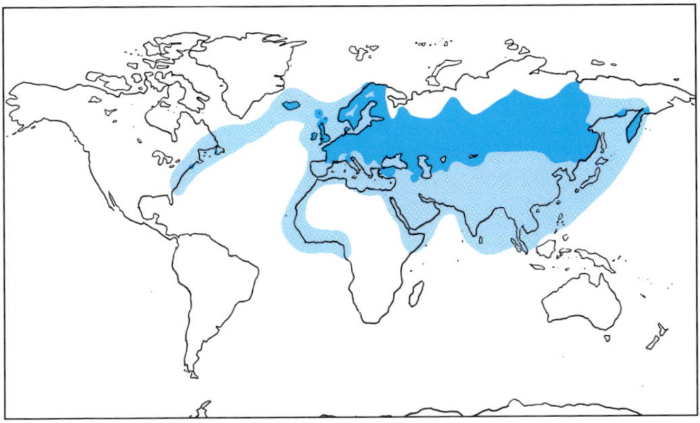

Identification One of the smaller gulls. In breeding plumage the adult has a chocolate-brown hood. There is an incomplete white ring around the eye while the bill and legs are red. The upperparts are pale grey with blackish wing tips. The underwing coverts are pale grey and outer primaries are dusky with black tips. Compare with Bonaparte's which has white outer primaries. In flight, shows a distinct white forewing at all ages. In non-breeding plumage has a white head with a dark smudge behind the eye.

Juvenile birds have dull orange legs and bill, the latter tipped with black. By end of second winter more or less as the adult bird.

Voice Noisy with various raucous calls, notably a harsh 'kwarp' or 'kawup'.

Habitat Breeds in a variety of situations including the edges of upland lakes and coastal marshes.

Food Scavenges for all manner of food, taking any small marine life it comes across. Inland, follows the plough eating worms and insect larvae

Range Breeds in Iceland, Faeroes, British Isles, where it is the most common breeding gull, then eastwards through central and northern Europe to Asia including shores of the Black and Caspian Seas and onwards to the Sea of Okhotsk and the Kamchatka Peninsula.

Movements After breeding scatters inland as well as around coasts.

A flock of foraging Black-headed Gulls in winter. Most birds show only the dark smudge behind the eye of their non-breeding plumage.

Slender-billed Gull

Larus genei 33–46cm (15–18in)

Nest	Scrape or shallow depression lined with some feathers or plant materials including seaweed
Egg clutch	Two or three
Egg colour	Pale cream, off-white or buff, blotched black or dark brown
Laid	May to June
Incubation	22 days
Fledging	Not known

Identification Although it never has a dark hood, it can be compared to the slightly smaller Black-headed Gull at all ages in both appearance and behaviour. However, the tail is longer than a Black-headed Gull, and it has a small head and long neck, which gives the appearance, when it is standing, that it is stretching its neck to see what is going on around it. Despite its

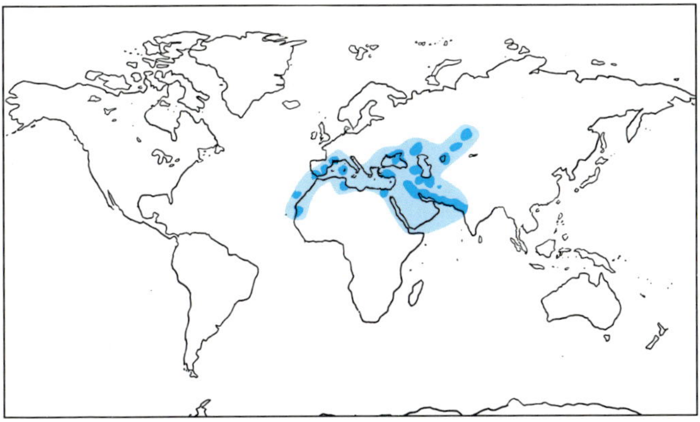

name, the bird's bill is not especially slender but is longer, more pointed and heavier than a Black-headed Gull's. At a distance, the adult bird's bill appears black though it is actually dark red. Like the Black-headed Gull, the forewing is white, a feature which could lead to the misidentification of immature birds where they occur together. In flight the neck has a 'drooped' look, with head and bill tilted downwards. The white iris is surrounded by a red orbital ring, and the feet and legs are red.
Voice Much like Black-headed Gull, but calls deeper, mellower and more nasal.
Habitat Sheltered lowland coasts with islands, beaches of shallow tidal water, meadows and moist grassland. Also brackish and freshwater lagoons in deltas or broad river valleys.
Food Small fish, crustaceans or insects, picking from the surface of the water, surface plunging or up-ending.
Range Breeds mainly in area of Black Sea and Caspian Sea. Also nests Sea of Azov, Egypt, Iraq, Sardinia, Turkey, the Persian Gulf and the Makran coast east of Karachi.
Movements After breeding, birds move away from colonies mostly to winter in the Mediterranean basin, Egypt and the Persian Gulf. Rare visitor to Britain.

An adult Slender-billed Gull is followed by an immature bird. Recorded in Britain on only five occasions, the most recent was at Cley, Norfolk in 1987.

Audouin's Gull

Larus audouinii 51cm (20in)

Nest A platform of grass and twigs with a shallow cup
Egg clutch Two to three
Egg colour Olive to olive-buff, marked with black and brown spots
Laid April to May
Incubation 28 days
Fledging 30–40 days

Identification Considered to be the world's rarest gull, it is between Herring Gull and Common Gull in size, and looks distinctly slender and tapered when at rest. The underparts and small-looking head, appear white at a distance, but the nape, sides of the breast, flanks, belly and upper rump are actually pale

grey. This colouring accentuates the white-headed, and white-tailed appearance of this bird at certain angles. The longish legs look black at a distance but are in fact olive green. Its main feature however is the bill. This is heavy looking, angular and bright red with a yellow tip separated by a black band. At long range, the yellow tip is not discernible and the bill appears blackish and blunt-ended. When standing, the adult bird shows a row of white spots on the black primaries of the folded wing. It is graceful in flight, and planes for long distances on its slim wings. Then the black primaries are most apparent, and form a wedge-shaped patch which is in marked contrast to the pale grey inner wing. At long distance the white primary tips are hardly noticeable. In second- and third-year birds, the black wedge extends to the carpal joint which, together with a pale grey crown, dark mask behind the eye, and brown upperparts, helps to distinguish it from Herring Gulls of similar ages.

Voice At nest site, noisy with various braying calls and goose-like sounds. At other times not very vocal, occasionally uttering a weak but harsh 'gi-erk'.

Habitat Nests on stony rocky slopes of islands, especially where bushes provide good ground cover.

Food Small fish picked from surface of the water.

Range As a breeding bird is confined to the Mediterranean Basin, mainly centred on the islands of Cyprus, Sardinia, Corsica and the Balearics, and some islets of western Italy.

Movements After nesting, most birds disperse in a westerly direction which takes them beyond Gibraltar where they winter off the Atlantic coasts of Morocco and the Spanish Sahara.

The Andouin's Gull favours well-vegetated rocky coasts of islands for its nest location.

Ring-billed Gull

Larus delawarensis 45–53cm (18–21in)

Nest	Built of grass, weed, and debris, sometimes decorated with feathers. Usually on ground but occasionally built in low trees. Colonial
Egg clutch	Three
Egg colour	Buffy, spotted brown and purplish grey
Laid	April to May
Incubation	26 days
Fledging	35 days

Identification A medium-sized species, this is a familiar gull across North America. The adult is pale grey above (a shade or two paler than Common Gull) with extensive black wing-tips marked by two white 'mirrors' on the outer primaries. The head is pure white in breeding plumage, but head, nape and sides of

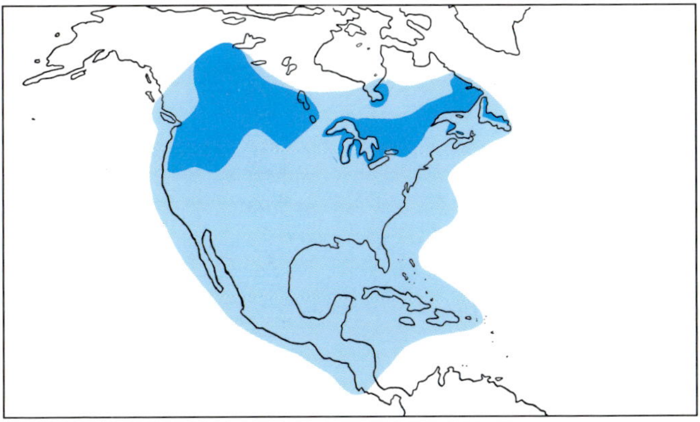

the neck are marked with diffuse pale brown blotches when in non-breeding plumage. The bill is yellow with a clear-cut subterminal band hence the name. It is usually larger with a 'heavier' tip than the tapered bill of Common Gull. The legs are yellowish. The yellow iris and, compared with Common Gull, the angled crown, give it a 'mean' expression. In first-year plumage Ring-billed Gull resembles a second-year Herring Gull, and care is needed to separate them. Look for neat dark centres to the tertials and wing coverts as compared with the rather messy, barred centres shown by Herring Gull. Second-year Ring-billed Gulls are much like adults.

Voice Usual call given in flight is 'kow-kow-kow'.

Habitat Nests on rocky, grassy or sandy islands with isolated shorelines and marshes. At other times haunts harbours, rubbish tips, sewage outfall. Forages the tideline and follows ships.

Food Scavenges all forms of marine life; also feeds on insects, worms, grubs, small rodents and occasionally birds' eggs.

Range Breeds widely across North America from Alberta to Labrador and Newfoundland, then southwards to Northern California, Illinois and New York. Some breed south-eastern British Columbia. Unknown in Britain before the first recorded instance in 1973, it has now become so frequent it is no longer considered a rarity. Noted in all months of the year with most in winter and a distinct peak in late March. Its recent relative abundance can be linked to its dramatic increase in eastern North America.

Movements After nesting, birds disperse over most of North America from British Columbia, the Great Lakes and Nova Scotia, south to Southern Mexico, the Gulf Coast, Florida, the Bahamas and the Greater Antilles with a few as far south as El Salvador.

Common Gull

Larus canus 40–46cm (16–18in)

Nest	Varies from a lined scrape to a substantial platform of grass and seaweed. Sometimes nest is well off ground on stone walls, and tree nesting takes place in some areas. Colonial
Egg clutch	Two or three
Egg colour	Pale blue or green to dark olive, blotched brown
Laid	May to June
Incubation	22–28 days
Fledging	35 days

Identification Smaller than somewhat similar Herring Gull, the noticeably rounder head, neck and body are pure white (head becomes streaked in winter) with a dark grey mantle. When at rest the wings project further beyond the tail than a Herring Gull, with the black primaries tipped white. The bill is yellow and the legs greenish (the Herring Gull's are pink). At close quarters a red orbital ring around the dark eye will be seen. The flight is light and buoyant and, compared with Herring Gull, the proportionately longer and thinner wings and the more prominent 'mirrors' on the outer two primaries are usually obvious. The young bird in flight is generally brownish, looking much darker than the adult on its underparts and showing pale edges to the feathering of the upperparts which give it a scaly

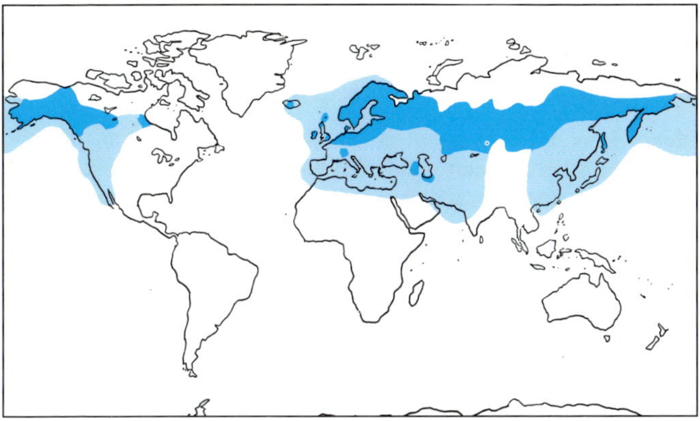

look. By its first winter the head and neck are whitish and the mantle, scapulars and back are clear grey. In flight shows white rump and black terminal band to tail. The bill is pink, tipped black. By the second year, head is whiter and less streaked and tail is now totally white; bill has become yellowish or green, tipped black. By third year bill is yellowish with black subterminal band, head is still streaked and at this age great care is needed to avoid misidentification as Ring-billed Gull. However, the Common Gull is more lightly built with shorter, tapered bill, shorter legs and darker mantle.

Voice A mewing call.

Habitat Breeds in a variety of locations including small rocky islets and islands; mainland grassy and rocky slopes; open moorland with small lochans; shingle bars or small islets on streams or rivers, and lakesides. At other times scavenges at tide-line and a variety of inland locations.

Food All manner of marine invertebrates, small fish; on land favours earthworms; will scavenge at rubbish tips and, like skuas, sometimes chases other birds to make them give up their food.

Range The nominate race breeds in Iceland and north-west Europe, including Britain and especially Scotland, south to Switzerland. The race *L. c. brachyrhynchus* breeds from Alaska, south along coast to British Columbia and into north-west Canada. The Siberian race *L. c. kamtschatschensis* breeds eastern Siberia.

Movements After breeding, disperses widely though where British birds go is not quite clear. However, it is believed the majority of the British and Irish wintering population come from Scandinavia, Denmark, Germany, with smaller numbers from Holland, the USSR and Iceland.

Herring Gull

Larus argentatus 56–66cm (22–26in)

Nest	Usually a mound of vegetation hollowed out in centre and lined with fine material, but will incorporate all sorts of material where available such as bits of plastic, old rope, fish netting
Egg clutch	Three
Egg colour	Olive with brown blotching
Laid	April to May
Incubation	28 days
Fledging	35–40 days

Identification An extremely variable species. There are 10 generally recognized subspecies. A medium-sized gull with white underparts, neck and head (streaked in winter), grey mantle and pink legs. Might be confused with Ring-billed Gull or possibly

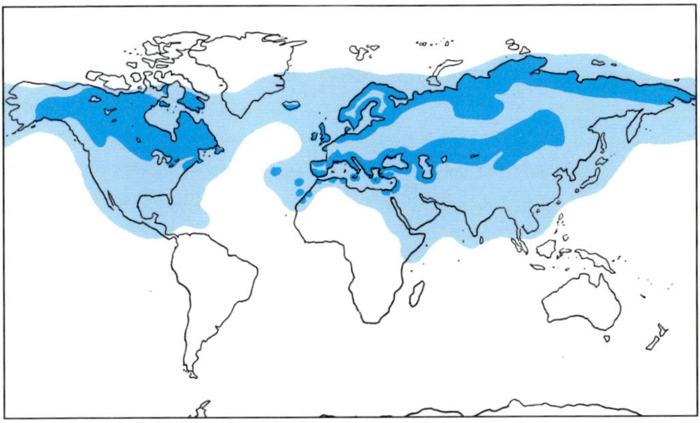

Common Gull, but is larger than both these species, broader-winged and with shallower forehead giving it a 'fierce' expression. During the four years it takes to reach maturity there is a steady transition from a heavily streaked, dull greyish-brown juvenile to a clean grey-white adult. At these early ages the legs are pinkish and the bill black. The adult bird's bill is yellow with a blood-red spot on the gonys. The race *L. a. michahellis*, which breeds in the Mediterranean basin north to Spain, has yellow legs.

Voice A variety of mewing, barking and laughing notes, including a frequently uttered 'kyow'. On breeding ground has a dry 'gah-gah-gah' call.

Habitat Breeds in sand dunes on shingle ridges, rocky islets and sea cliffs. In recent years has taken to nesting on flat rooftops of some coastal towns and cities.

Food Omnivorous, being particularly adept at exploiting man's waste; scavenges food from refuse tips and feeds on discarded waste in harbours and docks. Forages along seashore for small fish and crustaceans. Inland, it takes worms, insect larvae and vegetable matter.

Range Circumpolar as a breeding bird, nesting as far north as the Arctic Circle in North America, northern Europe, (common in Britain), eastwards through northern Siberia. Also found in southern Europe eastwards through Mediterranean into Asia.

Movements Most migratory within the northerly population, although Icelandic and North American birds appear to be mainly sedentary. Immature birds tend to wander further afield than adults. The 'yellow-legged' (*L. a. michahellis*) race seems to be spreading its range northwards. Certainly there has been a definite increase in numbers of sightings in Britain in recent years.

Lesser Black-backed Gull

Larus fuscus 51–61cm (20–24in)

Nest	A substantial heap of grass, seaweed and other local materials, often well hidden in vegetation. At times a sparsely lined scrape in a more open situation
Egg clutch	Two to three
Egg colour	Pale blue or green to dark brown, spotted blackish brown
Laid	May to June
Incubation	28 days
Fledging	30–40 days

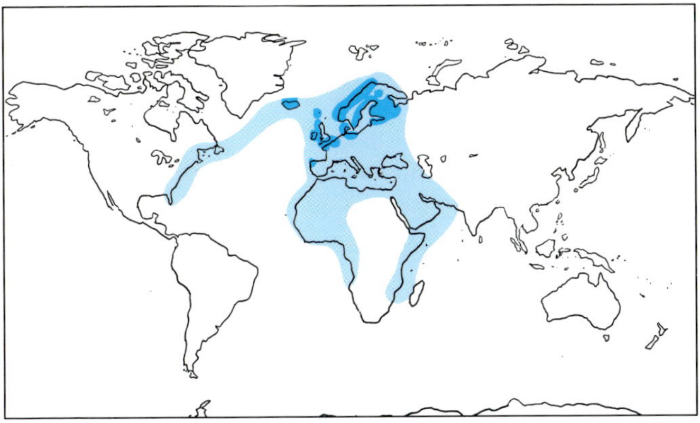

Identification The adult has an immaculate slate-grey back and slate-grey wings with black and white tips while the head and underparts are pure white. (In winter head and neck are heavily streaked with grey). The yellow bill has a red spot on the gonys, while the yellow eye is ringed with red. The legs are yellow though in winter these can look greyish or pink. In flight looks slim with proportionally larger narrower, more pointed wings than Herring Gull. Develops to maturity over four years: the first-winter bird is much like a first-winter Herring Gull but the head and belly are usually pale with underparts more contrasting. The bill of the young bird is always entirely black. Second-winter plumage is again similar to second-winter Herring Gull but is darker on the back and at this age legs are often yellow. By third winter legs are yellow, rarely pink, and some brown remains on the wings. The bill is yellow with a dark smudge on the tip.
Voice A variety of calls similar to Herring Gull.
Habitat Breeds at undisturbed coastal localities with sand dunes or on relatively flat unbroken grassy slopes. Colonial.
Food An omnivorous bird, taking any marine life. Also feeds on carrion and scavenges for all manner of food on rubbish tips.
Range The nominate race *L. f. fuscus* breeds in the Baltic and Northern Norway, while *L. f. intermedius* breeds in southern Norway, west Sweden and Denmark. The British race *L. f. graellsii* breeds southern Ireland, the Faeroes and British Isles.
Movements After nesting, disperses on a broad southerly front, some reaching the Red Sea, Nigeria and Kenya. In North America there is now a regular but small population passing through Newfoundland and wintering south to Florida.

The dark wings of this Lesser Black-backed Gull identify it as belonging to the nominate race, *Larus f. fuscus.*

Iceland Gull

Larus glaucoides 58–64cm (23–25in)

Nest A loose construction of seaweed, grass and mosses placed on a flat roomy ledge, often found with Kittiwakes
Egg clutch Two to three
Egg colour Buff to olive-brown
Laid May to July
Incubation Unknown
Fledging Unknown

Identification Smaller than the similar-plumaged Glaucous Gull. In adult plumage, all white except for back and wings which are very pale grey. The legs are pale flesh-pink, while the bill is yellow with an orange spot on the gonys. At close range, a brick-red orbital ring can be seen around the yellow eye.

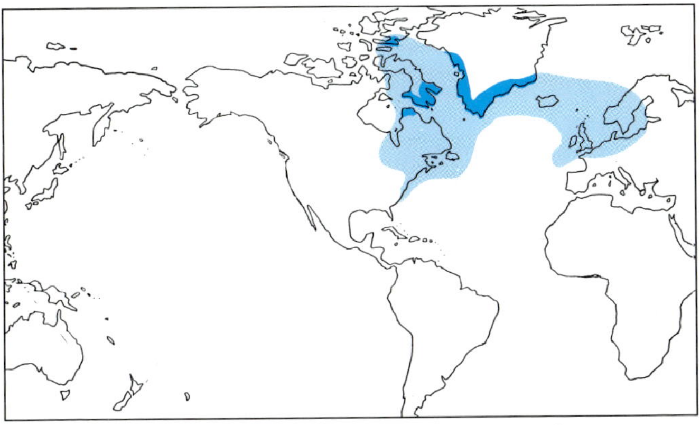

Approximately the size of a Herring Gull, the bill is smaller and less heavy. Compared with Glaucous Gull, the wings extend well beyond the tail at rest, giving it a long slender look. The flight is also much more buoyant and the wings appear relatively longer than Glaucous Gull. Takes four years to reach maturity. In their first winter Iceland Gulls are generally buff to white with wing-tips irregularly washed with brown. The eye is dark, the bill black and the legs greyish. The fine and usually even pattern of grey-brown markings is only visible at close range, but in flight there is a distinct white terminal band found in the tail. In each succeeding year the plumage becomes whiter, the pale grey mantle forms and the colour of the bill and legs becomes brighter.

Voice Similar to Herring Gull but shriller.

Habitat Rocky coasts with high steep cliffs during breeding season, occasionally choosing lower cliffs. Offshore stacks and islands. Coastal at other times, but can also occur inland.

Food Mainly fish, but also molluscs and crustaceans. Will scavenge and feed on carrion.

Range Breeds extensively in Greenland and also in North America from Ellesmere Island south to Baffin Island.

Movements After nesting some birds move to Europe, wintering from Iceland to the Faeroes and Norway with some occasionally seen south to Sweden, the Baltic, northern France, northern Belgium, the Netherlands and British Isles. In a normal year southern Britain and Ireland may have a winter population of possibly a hundred birds, scattered around the region, particularly in Scotland.

An adult Iceland Gull.

Glaucous Gull

Larus hyperboreus 66–77cm (26–30in)

Nest	A substantial pile of seaweed, other vegetation or locally obtained debris, lined with finer materials and maybe a few feathers
Egg clutch	Two or three, rarely four
Egg colour	Buffy to olive, blotched dark brown
Laid	May or early June
Incubation	28 days
Fledging	45–50 days

Identification A thick set powerful barrel-chested bird, size varies from that of Great Black-backed Gull to approximately Herring Gull size. Heavier build and fiercer expression, due to massive bill and flatter crown, help distinguish from Iceland Gull. The adult is all white except for very pale grey back and wings. The wings are relatively shorter than Iceland Gull and do not project so far beyond the tail. The yellow bill with the red spot on the gonys is stout and somewhat larger than Iceland Gull. At close range a yellow eye ring is detectable though in winter this is practically colourless. The legs are flesh coloured. At a

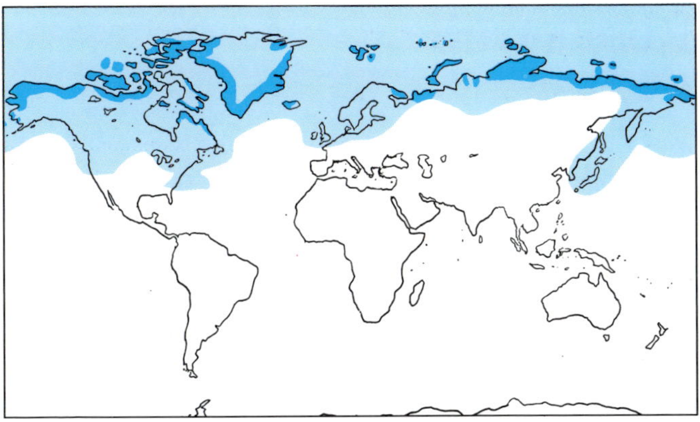

distance the juvenile looks a uniform coffee-colour, always much paler looking than other large immature gulls. At close quarters it will be seen that the plumage comprises fine, wavy, buff-coloured, barred and mottled feathers. The first-winter bird which also appears coffee-coloured has a diagnostic flesh-coloured bill with a clearly delineated black tip. In its second winter the black in the bill is less distinct, with the extreme tip becoming white, while the base is often yellowish. By the second summer the bill has become a pinkish yellow with a dusky tip. In its third year, bill and legs are almost as the adult without red gonys. Each year the plumage becomes whiter until full adult plumage is achieved in fourth year.

Voice Resembles Herring Gull but higher pitched.

Habitat Breeds on coastal islands and along cliff faces of Arctic and sub-Arctic coasts. Also nests on islands in freshwater lakes, usually near to coast.

Food Omnivorous, preying on other birds, their eggs and young. Will regularly take such species as Little Auk on nesting ground. Scavenges tideline, eating any carrion it finds.

Range Circumpolar, breeds mainly north of Arctic Circle from Alaska east across Arctic Canada to Greenland, Iceland, Spitsbergen and in northern Europe from Murmansk along shores of USSR to Wrangel Island and the Bering Strait.

Movements Birds breeding in Canadian Arctic and west Greenland mainly sedentary, but some move south into eastern America. The eastern Greenland population appears more migratory and largely moves to Iceland; some no doubt reach Ireland and Britain. There is a regular winter population in the Shetlands where in some years up to 100 birds may occur.

Ross's Gull

Rhodostethia rosea 30–32cm (12–13in)

Nest Grass and leaves sometimes with a base of willow or other twigs
Egg clutch Three
Egg colour Pale buff, blotched dark brown
Laid June
Incubation 28 days
Fledging 43 days

Identification In breeding plumage this bird is one of the most delightful of all gulls. It has a pearl grey back and wings and the white underparts, rump and tail are suffused with a soft rosy pink colour. Around the head there is a narrow black ring; this is usually absent in winter, when it is replaced by a dusky crescent extending from in front to below the eye, and a dusky mark on

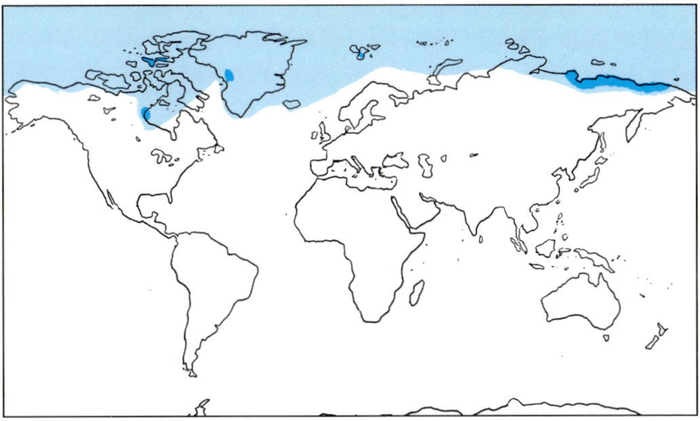

the ear coverts. The bill is very small, thin and black, and the feet and legs are bright red. The wings are very long and pointed and they project well beyond the tail when the bird is at rest. In this posture the round head, small bill and short legs give a dove-like impression. Although not always easy to see in the field, no other gull has a similar longish, wedge-shaped tail. This is a useful distinction from the Little Gull, which as an immature bird shows a similar striking 'M'-shaped pattern across the wings as does a first year Ross's Gull. In addition, at this age only the tip of the central tail feathers are black whereas a juvenile Little Gull shows a complete black band along the tip of its tail. A Ross's Gull has a very bouncy flight, at times hovers, and frequently trails legs in water. Will also feed in wader fashion along the shore.

Voice Variable high-pitched calls which are more melodious than other gulls with a typical bubbling 'e-wo, e-wo, e-wo'.

Habitat Breeds in well-wooded marshy valleys, also Arctic tundra. At other times ranges the Arctic oceans.

Food Small fish, crustaceans and insects. On breeding is especially insectivorous.

Range Confined to High Arctic, main breeding area north-east Siberia, USSR from Kharanga River to Kolyina delta region. Also, some breed Bathurst Island near Churchill in Canada. Winters across the Arctic.

Movements Returns to breeding grounds late May or early June. After nesting July/August, some move eastwards towards Chukchi and Bering Seas to Alaska. Others move westwards along Siberian coast through the Kara Sea to Franz Josef Land and Spitsbergen where it is believed many birds winter. Has almost become an annual visitor to northern British waters in recent years.

Great Black-backed Gull

Larus marinus 71–79cm (28–31in)

Nest	A large pile of grass, seaweed and any other handy vegetation, along with all manner of litter. The cup is often lined with finer materials
Egg clutch	Two to three
Egg colour	Pale buff to olive brown, blotched dark brown
Laid	May
Incubation	26–28 days
Fledging	42–56 days

Identification Largest of the gulls, its white head, neck and underparts, black mantle and wings with bold white tips, pinkish legs and huge yellow bill with red-tipped gonys make it an easy bird to identify in full breeding plumage. Close views reveal a

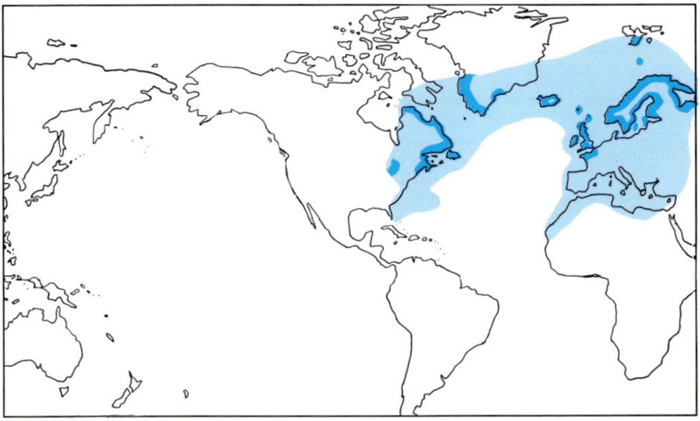

cold calculating white eye and a red orbital ring which give it a fearsome look. Similar in non-breeding plumage except for a few dark flecks on nape.

In juvenile plumage, shows a chequered pattern of blackish brown on the upperparts and whitish underparts. The legs are a dull flesh colour while the bill is black. In first winter the head is much whiter, while the upperparts and upperwing coverts are more distinctly patterned black and white than first-winter Herring Gull. By second year, the whiteness of the head and uniformity of the dark mantle is intensified, and by third year has almost assumed adult plumage, though not until its fourth or fifth year does it become fully mature.

Voice Usually either a deep-clipped 'owk' or longer 'ow-ow-ow-ow' calls.

Habitat Nests on small islets or grassy slopes of isolated mainland areas. At other times coastal, haunting estuaries, bays and the open sea, being more marine than most other gulls and less common inland.

Food Omnivorous, eating almost anything that comes its way along the shoreline or elsewhere. Eats other birds, particularly Puffins, including eggs and young whenever it can.

Range In the north Atlantic nests around Greenland, Iceland, Spitsbergen and the Faeroes. In western Europe it extends from Murmansk in the USSR round the coasts of Finland, Norway and Sweden to the Baltic Sea, the British Isles and north-west France.

Movements British breeding birds are mainly sedentary but the Russian and Scandinavian populations move south to Britain, France and the Mediterranean in the winter.

An adult Great Black-backed Gull.

Kittiwake

Rissa tridactyla 39–46cm (15½–18in)

Nest	A neat construction of compacted seaweed and sometimes grass and moss, attached to the sheer rock face. It has quite a deep cup
Egg clutch	One to three
Egg colour	Pale blue grey to light brown, marked with darker brown
Laid	May to June
Incubation	21–24 days
Fledging	43 days

Identification Generally resembles a Common Gull but is slightly smaller and has solid black tips to the wings. The head, neck and underparts are white and back and wings coverts deep grey. The legs are black and the bill yellow. The dark eye softens the expression giving a gentle look. Its flight is bounding with a quicker wing action than other grey-backed gulls. The tail is slightly forked (more noticeable in the immature when also tipped with black). When feeding, takes food from surface of water or plunge dives like a tern. The young birds have a distinctive plumage pattern which is most discernible in flight

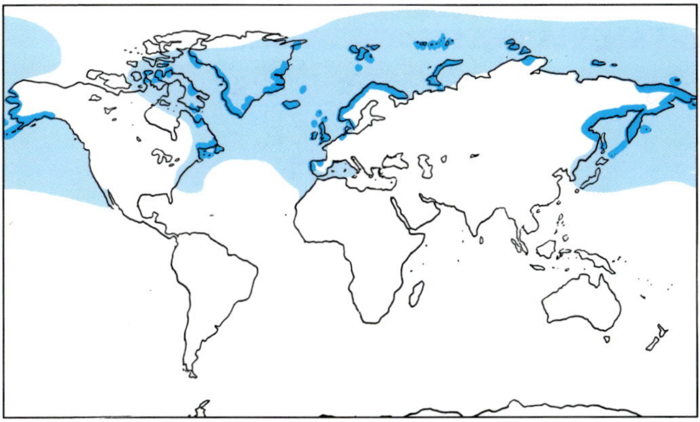

and this is retained until their second winter. At these ages a pattern of black diagonal bars in the wing form an 'M' similar to Little Gull, but unlike the latter species also shows a black cervical collar. When seen together, the larger size of the Kittiwake makes separation easy.

Voice Proclaims its name with an incessant 'kitti-wa-ak, kitti-wa-ak' at nest site. Silent at other times.

Habitat Precipitous sea cliff faces when nesting, though in recent times some have taken to using riverside buildings. After breeding, spends most of the year far out to sea.

Food Small fish, crustaceans, worms, molluscs, insects, mostly takes food from surface but sometimes dives like a tern. Frequently follows ships, feeding in the wake.

Range There are two races. The nominate race, *R. t. tridactyla*, breeds along coast of Arctic Canada including Prince Leopold Island, Bylot Island and Baffin Island, northern Labrador, the Gulf of St Lawrence, Newfoundland and Nova Scotia, and in Greenland, Iceland, Spitsbergen, Jan Mayen, the Faeroes, Novaya Zemlya and along the north coast of USSR. In northern Europe it breeds from Murmansk south to Norway, the British Isles, the Baltic and northern France. The race *R. t. pollicaris* breeds in the USSR from north-east Siberia south to Kamchatka and Commander Islands then eastwards through Bering Strait to the Aleutian Islands.

Movements After nesting, birds disperse to sea. In the east Atlantic most remain north of 40°N, but some reach the Mediterranean. During periods of gales, particularly in October and November, thousands of Kittiwakes might be seen moving along the south-western and eastern coasts of Britain. In recent years observation has shown a regular small passage of birds across inland Britain in spring and autumn.

Ivory Gull

Pagophila eburnea 40–46cm (16–18in)

Nest	A bulky structure mostly built of seaweed with a lining of grass and perhaps a few feathers
Egg clutch	Two
Egg colour	Buff to pale, blotched dark olive to black
Laid	June to July
Incubation	24–25 days
Fledging	35 days

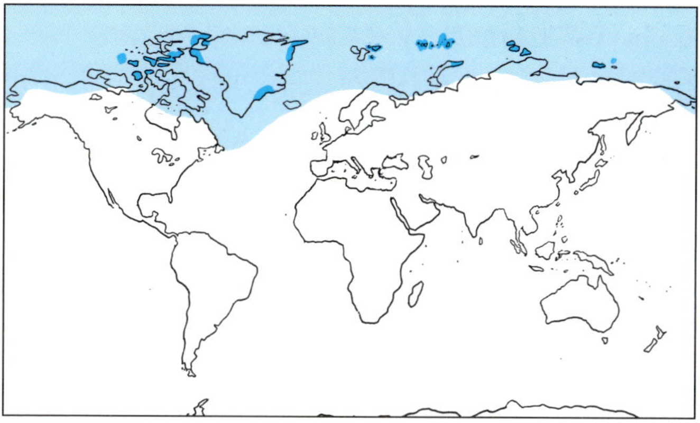

Identification Wholly ivory white, hence the name. At rest its domed crown, plump body and short black legs give it a distinct pigeon-like appearance which is accentuated by its 'waddling' gait. There is a short, dove-like bill which is slate-blue at base, becoming pale yellow, tipped with red. The iris is black-brown with a red orbital ring. The dark eye gives it a deceptively gentle expression for it is a quarrelsome and aggressive bird. First-winter birds show irregular grey smudges on the face and chin, often with a small dark crescent around the eye. There is also a light sprinkling of spots on the underparts and sometimes the upperparts; the primaries have black tips and the tail has a very black terminal band. In flight, looks long-winged and heavy-bodied, but is nevertheless buoyant and graceful, often flying with legs trailing, when it reveals yellow shafts to the primaries.
Voice Shrill, dissyllabic call, not unlike Common Tern.
Habitat Nests on offshore islands but also steep cliff faces.
Food Mainly fish and invertebrates obtained by dipping surface or plunge diving, but frequently scavenges polar bear kills.
Range Breeds to the north of the July isotherm of 5°C and includes part of the Canadian Arctic, Northern Greenland, Spitsbergen, Franz Josef Land, Novaya Zemlya and Severnaya Zemlya.

A vagrant to Britain and Europe most sightings have been in the months of November and December. Since 1958 there have been around 30 records in Britain with a decrease in frequency over the last two decades.

Movements After nesting, birds disperse to winter within the northern Atlantic and the Chukchi and Bering Seas. They move with the pack-ice and drift generally southwards.

Gull-billed Tern

Gelochelidon nilotica 35–43cm (14–17in)

Nest	A scrape in dried mud, sand or gravel, lined with pieces of grass and at times bits of debris
Egg clutch	Two to four
Egg colour	Pale yellow, buff or cream, speckled blackish or brown
Laid	May
Incubation	22–23 days
Fledging	20–35 days

Identification The Gull-billed Tern is about the size of a Black headed Gull, with broader wings. It has a blunt, wholly black, gull-like bill. Plumage is typically tern-like, having underparts white and upperparts ash grey. The crown and nape are black, which is much deeper than similar-looking Sandwich Tern but without the hint of a crest so obvious in the other bird. The

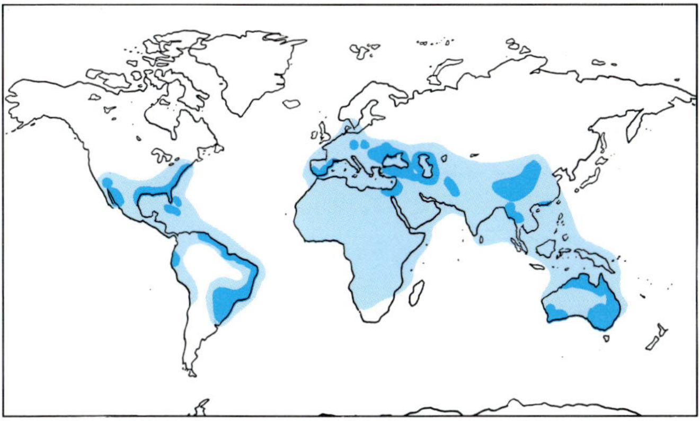

upperwing is coloured as upperpart, underwing white, showing a noticeably dark trailing edge to both the upper and under primaries. The silver grey rump and tail give it quite a different look to the Sandwich Tern which has a wholly white rump and tail. At rest, its relatively long black legs are a feature of the species. In winter develops white crown with dark streaks. A solid-looking bird, its gull-like flight, however, lacks the grace and buoyancy of other terns. Juvenile has pale edgings to feathers on upperparts and the bill is brownish.

Voice A rather nasal 'rhaa-rhaa gahak-id'.

Habitat Occurs inland as well as on the coast. Nests in marshes, on lakesides, and at times can be seen feeding over fields.

Food Terrestrial and aquatic insects, including grasshoppers, crickets, dragonflies. Also takes worms, frogs, lizards and small mammals.

Range In Europe, breeds discontinuously in Denmark, Holland, Spain and southern France, and from eastern Europe across Asia Minor and eastwards to Mongolia and the Punjab. Also breeds in north and East Africa.

Movements After nesting, the European population moves south of the Sahara to winter in Africa. At such times and on its return in the spring some birds noted in Britain, mainly May or September.

Two Gull-billed Terns at rest showing their relatively long black legs and blunt, wholly black, gull-like bill, both distinctive identifying features.

Caspian Tern

Sterna caspia 48–59cm (19–23in)

Nest A scrape in the ground on shingle bank, dry mud or sand, sometimes lined with pieces of rotting vegetation
Egg clutch Two or three
Egg colour Buff coloured, blotched dark brown
Laid May to June
Incubation 25 days
Fledging 28–35 days

Identification A huge tern, as big as a medium-sized gull. The adult in breeding plumage has a black cap, pearl-grey upperparts and white underparts, while in flight the wing-tips show a large dusky area. The most notable feature however is the massive

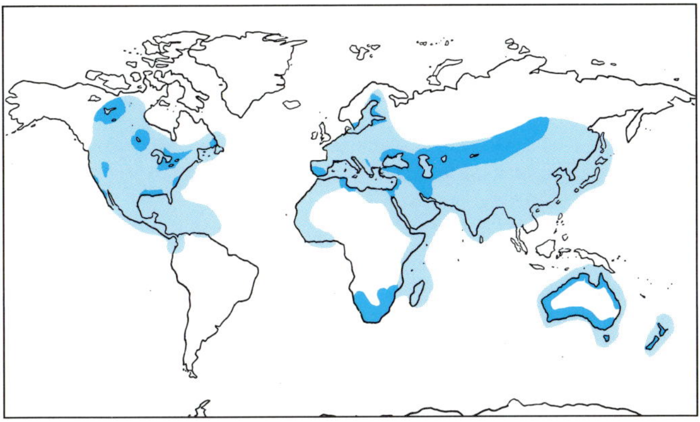

dagger-like, blood-red bill. In full breeding plumage this generally has a black tip, though can be yellow, orange or white. The fairly long legs are black. In non-breeding plumage the black cap becomes streaked with white, but never shows a fully white forehead as Royal Tern. The Royal Tern is also slightly smaller, and has an orange-red bill without dark tip.

Voice A deep rasping 'kra-kra-kraa-uh'.

Habitat For breeding: sea coasts, estuaries or shores of inland lakes and seas. Occasionally rocky islands.

Food Makes dramatic plunge dive for food, often disappearing completely below the surface. Fish of all sorts, especially herring, and on occasions invertebrates, and eggs and young of other birds.

Range In Europe there have been decreases in the breeding range of this species and it is now either extinct as a nesting bird or nests less regularly than it did in Denmark, Germany and Rumania. The same is true in Tunisia. In contrast, there have been some increases in numbers in Sweden, Finland and Estonia. Nests southern Spain, the area of the northern Black Sea eastwards across Asia to the Caspian Sea, Persian Gulf and into eastern Siberia.

Movements Migration still not fully understood but generally northern breeding population winter in the tropics and those nearer the Equator are probably sedentary. During its migration a few reach Britain most years, generally occurring during the summer months.

An adult Caspian Tern in non-breeding plumage with crown and forehead finely streaked with white markings. The huge carrot-like bill with the black tip is always diagnostic.

Royal Tern

Sterna maxima 46–53cm (18–21in)

Nest	A depression in the sand with a few bits of shoreline debris added during incubation
Egg clutch	One, rarely two
Egg colour	White to medium brown, blotched red and brown
Laid	May to June
Incubation	30–36 days
Fledging	28–35 days

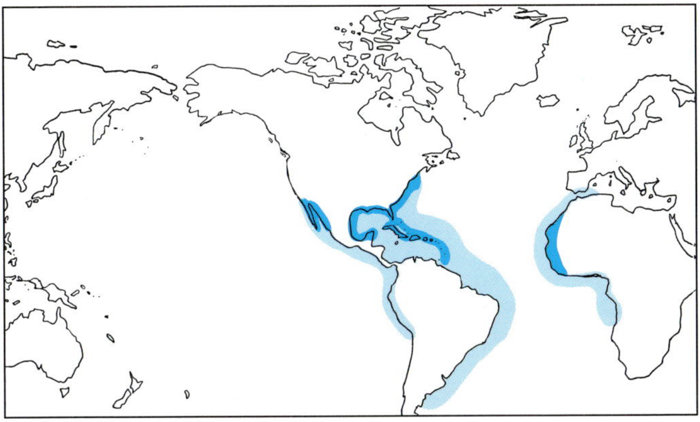

Identification The second largest tern, about the size of a Common Gull, its general appearance is much the same as other terns with dark cap, pearl-grey back, white underparts, rump and tail. However, the full black crown of breeding plumage is acquired but briefly in the early part of the nesting period and for most of the year the bird's forehead and lores are white. The bill, which is almost as long as the head, comes to a much finer point than a Caspian Tern's and is usually deep orange in colour and never shows a dusky subterminal band as does the other bird. The legs are black. Flight is swift and strong, showing long, pointed wings and deeply pointed tail. Catches its food in the usual tern-like manner, by plunge diving.
Voice Alarm call a hard 'keet-keet' or 'krit-krit' and similar notes to Sandwich Tern.
Habitat Along coasts and on inshore and offshore islands, favouring beaches, estuaries, lagoons and mangrove coasts.
Food Fish, also favours crabs and other crustacea.
Range Breeds North America, Caribbean and north-west Africa. North American birds winter south to Ecuador and Argentina. African birds winter south to Angola.
Movements A vagrant to Britain, it has been recorded on only four occasions, all since 1954, with the latest in 1979.

A group of Royal Terns nesting on a Florida shoreline in early spring. Some have totally black caps while some show white foreheads.

Lesser-crested Tern

Sterna bengalensis 38–43cm (15–17in)

Nest	Shallow scrape without lining
Egg clutch	Three
Egg colour	White, cream or buff invariably spotted or speckled black or dark brown
Laid	June to November
Incubation	21–26 days
Fledging	32–35 days

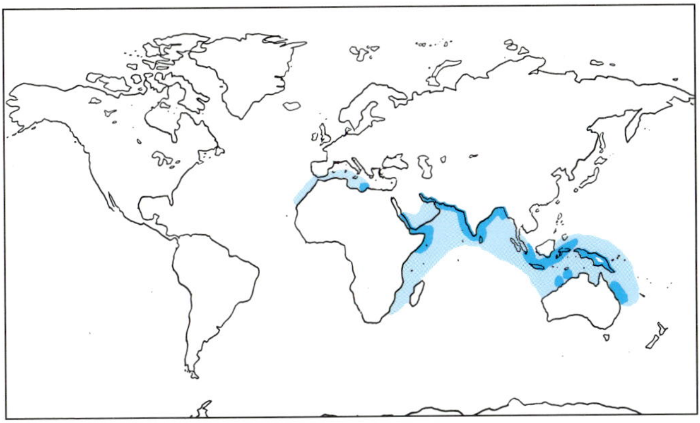

Identification Slightly smaller than Sandwich Tern, and much smaller than Royal Tern. Colour pattern similar to other terns with upperparts pale bluish-grey to deep steel-grey (dependent on geographical location of population in question). Underparts white. The black cap normally extends from base of bill to nape, with face, chin and throat white. In non-breeding and immature plumage, the forehead is white. The relatively large pointed bill is usually orange, though smaller and paler than the bill of the Royal Tern, the Sandwich Tern has a black bill with yellow tip. The legs are black. Flight fast and graceful. Plunge dives for food and will also take prey from surface of the water. Also readily settles on water to rest.
Voice Calls 'kek-kereck'.
Habitat Favours flat, sandy beaches for nesting, especially on low lying islands, also bare sand spits, flat rocks or coral reefs. Feeds inshore and also forages far out to sea.
Food Small fish and crustaceans.
Range Mainly found throughout the Indian and Pacific Oceans with subspecies breeding in the Mediterranean, Red Sea, East Africa, Persian Gulf east to Singapore, the Malay archipelago, and Australia.
Movements Sedentary in some parts of its range, but Mediterranean population moves mainly west in autumn to Algeria, Morocco and occasionally Gibraltar, with most believed to winter off coast of north-west Africa. Red Sea birds disperse southwards reaching Mozambique, Natal and South Africa. There have been a handful of sightings of Lesser-crested Terns in Britain, since it was first recorded in 1982, including birds returning to Dawlish Warren during the period from 1985 to 1988.

Sandwich Tern

Sterna sandvicensis 40–45cm (16–18in)

Nest	A scrape in the ground
Egg clutch	One or two
Egg colour	Yellowish, streaked black, brown and dark grey
Laid	May
Incubation	25 days
Fledging	28–30 days

Identification A largish tern, its flight is less buoyant and more gull-like than smaller terns and the tail is less deeply forked than many. The upperparts are pale grey, the underparts white and the crown black. The bill is black with a yellow tip and the legs are black. At rest while in breeding plumage, it will be seen that the black cap extends from the base of the bill to the nape and the crown feathers are elongated to form a distinctive crest, which is

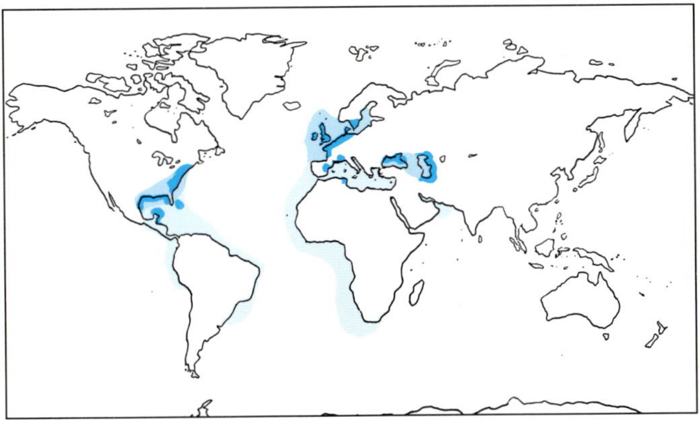

more obvious when the bird gets excited during courtship. In non-breeding plumage, the front of the crown turns white – this is often assumed even while the birds are still nesting – and by September or October the whole of the head has developed a streaky appearance. Juveniles are similar to non-breeding adults, but lack yellow tip to the bill.

Confusion most likely with Gull-billed Tern which lacks yellow tip to bill. At a distance, Sandwich Tern looks slimmer and more rakish.

Voice A far-carrying grating 'kirrick'; when alarmed utters an incessant 'krit' or 'krik' note.

Habitat For nesting, favours low-lying sand or shingly beaches, but sometimes chooses rocky coasts or islands.

Food Fish and especially sand eels.

Range Breeds in isolated colonies in Britain and Ireland and along the north European and Baltic coasts, particularly Holland, Germany, Denmark and Sweden. Some breed France. Has nested irregularly Italy, Spain and Tunisia. Also breeds around shores of the Black Sea and the southern and eastern shores of the Sea of Azov.

Movements After breeding, the European population moves south to winter from Portugal to South Africa, but most are to be found along the tropical west African coast. The Black Sea population mainly winters in the west Mediterranean, while those from the Caspian Sea area spread to the Persian Gulf east to the Indian Ocean.

Erratic at times in its breeding behaviour, whole colonies of Sandwich Terns will desert their nesting areas for no apparent reason than to begin again elsewhere.

Roseate Tern

Sterna dougallii 35–43cm (14–17in)

Nest	Shallow scrape in sand with little or no lining, but pieces of grass added during incubation
Egg clutch	Two
Egg colour	Creamy buff, blotched black-brown
Laid	Early June
Incubation	23 days
Fledging	27–30 days

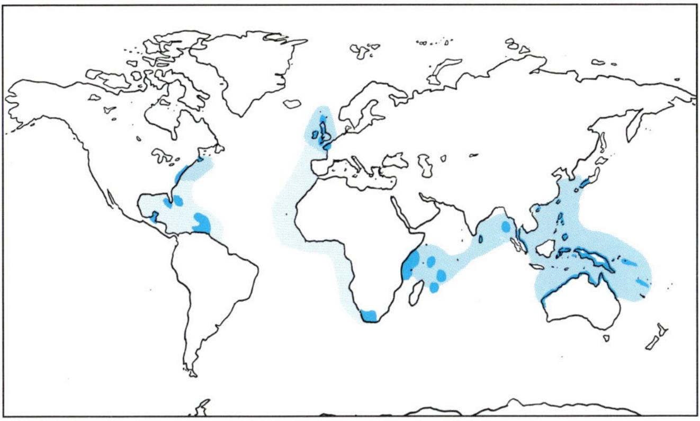

Identification Similar to Common Tern or Arctic Tern in size, but can be distinguished from them by its very white appearance, slimmer body, and noticeably long 'whipping' tail streamers.

Like other terns, there is a black cap which is long but rather shallow, while the back and wings are pearl-grey or pale blue-grey, noticeably paler than Common Tern. Another distinction is the bill which is long, pointed and usually almost wholly black, except for the base which is dull red in summer. The legs are red. Additionally, when the bird is at rest it will be seen that the tail streamers extend far beyond the folded wing, whereas on the Common Tern they just reach the folded wing tips, and on the Arctic Tern extend only slightly beyond them. The distinctive rosy tinge from which the bird gets its name only shows for a short period in the early part of the breeding season.

Voice A drawn out rasping 'aaak', also a characteristic 'chu-ick' and a long chattering 'kekekekekek' after defending territory.

Habitat For nesting, usually chooses sand dunes with marram grass. More sea-going than some other terns and rarely noted overland at migration times.

Food Small fish, especially sand eels.

Range Globally a widespread breeding bird, with its European stronghold in Britain and Ireland, though total breeding population is probably no more than 400 pairs. There are small colonies in Brittany, with sporadic breeding in Denmark and Germany.

Movements After nesting moves south to winter off the coasts of north-west Africa.

The graceful buoyant flight of the Roseate Tern makes it probably the most attractive member of all the Sternidae family.

Common Tern

Sterna hirundo 32–38cm (12½in)

Nest	Scrape or hollow in sand or shingle, lined with varying amounts of local materials. At times in tideline debris, and on sunken boats, old piers
Egg clutch	Two to four
Egg colour	Cream to dark brown, blotched dark brown, sometimes pale green or blue, unmarked
Laid	May to June
Incubation	22–26 days
Fledging	28 days

Identification A graceful, medium-sized tern with white underparts, pale grey back, black cap, red legs and a red bill with a black tip. Has long, pointed wings and forked tail with projecting streamers of moderate length in breeding plumage.

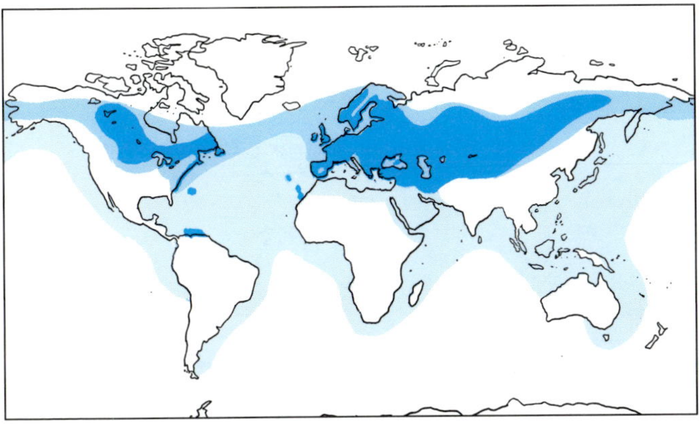

Similar to Arctic Tern and often difficult to separate, particularly in flight, but when viewed from below the innermost primaries of Common Tern show up as a translucent panel or 'window', whereas all primaries are translucent on Arctic Tern. When at rest differences between the two species are more obvious: the legs are slightly longer and the folded wing of the Common Tern can be seen to extend to virtually the same length as the tail. In non-breeding plumage, forehead becomes white and crown streaked, tail lacks streamers and bill is blackish. The juvenile is brownish above and white below with a mostly dark bill and a white forehead. In flight shows a prominent dark shoulder bar, as do all birds in non-breeding plumage.

Voice A long, grating 'keeeee-yaah'. Also a frequently uttered 'kik-kik-kik'.

Habitat Breeds along coastal dunes, salt marshes, and also on the shores of lakes or along rivers.

Food Small fish and sand eels.

Range Globally nests throughout most of Europe, Asia and North America. In Britain mostly breeds along the west coast of Scotland, but also favours East Anglia, parts of the south coast, also Isles of Scilly, Anglesey and Isle of Man. A fair number also breed inland in north-east Scotland and the east Midlands. It is also found in suitable localities in Ireland.

Movements After breeding, generally moves south to winter along western seaboard of Africa, mainly in the region of West Africa.

A Common Tern, incubating its eggs, calls to its mate.

Arctic Tern

Sterna paradisaea 33–38cm (13–15in)

Nest	A scrape in sand or shingle or turf lined with marram grass or shells
Egg clutch	Two, sometimes three
Egg colour	Stone, blotched dark brown
Laid	May to June
Incubation	22 days
Fledging	21–28 days

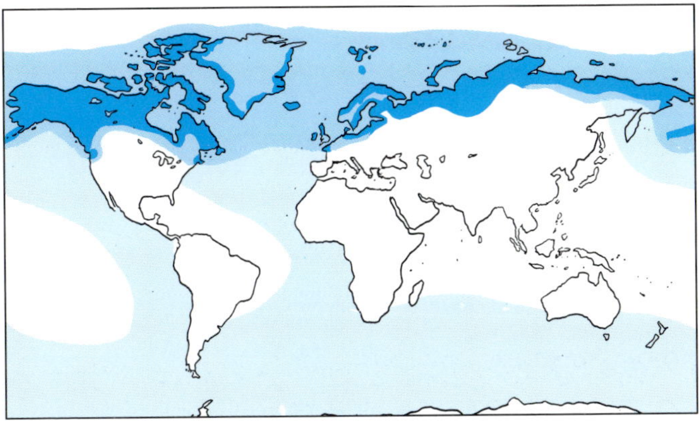

Identification Very similar to Common Tern with white underparts, grey back and black cap. However, the Arctic Tern has longer tail streamers and relatively slimmer wings and its flight is generally more buoyant and airy. In breeding plumage the Arctic Tern has greyer-looking underparts which make the contrasting white cheeks a more prominent feature. All the primaries on this species are translucent when viewed from below. At rest, the folded wing does not reach the end of the tail, and the red legs are much shorter than Common Tern. The wholly blood-red bill should verify identification. The juvenile is not so brownish overall as Common Tern and the shoulder bar is less distinct. The tail lacks streamers. The forehead is white and crown and nape blackish. In non-breeding plumage, adult birds have white forehead, a streaked crown and blackish bill.
Voice A high whistling 'kee kee' rising in pitch, also notes similar to Common Tern.
Habitat Similar to Common Tern but inclined to be more maritime and does not normally nest any great distance from the coast.
Food Small fish and especially sand eels.
Range Circumpolar in its breeding distribution, is to be found nesting in Iceland, the Faeroes, Britain (mostly in north) and Ireland, with small numbers in France and then from Baltic Scandinavia east including Spitsbergen and northern USSR to the Bering Sea.
Movements Makes some of the lengthiest migrations of all bird species, moving from the Arctic to the Antarctic and back again within a year. In Europe, passage mostly coastal or offshore to join North Sea and Atlantic flyway southwards. Regularly noted on passage in Britain, particularly in the autumn.

Forster's Tern

Sterna forsteri 35–41cm (14–16in)

Nest	On floating vegetation, small islets. Sometimes a large well-built and elaborate structure of dead sedge and grass with a neat cup woven in the top
Egg clutch	Three, sometimes four or five
Egg colour	Buff to olive-buff, blotched dark brown and purplish grey
Laid	June to July
Incubation	23–25 days
Fledging	28 days

Identification In breeding plumage very similar to Common Tern in having an orange-red bill tipped with black. Structurally, it differs subtly in its heavier bill, longer legs and longer tail streamers which extend beyond the tail when perched. The most important distinctions, however, are the snow white underparts, grey tail with narrow white sides, the paler, silvery, inner primaries which often appear strikingly lighter than the rest of the wing, and less black on the outer wing. In non-breeding plumage from August onwards (assumed rather earlier than

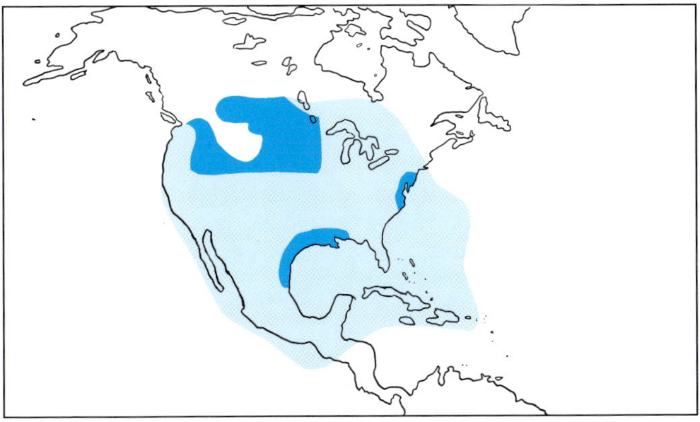

Common Tern or Arctic Tern), loses black cap which is replaced by a black mask through the eye. Although there may be some streaking over the nape, the eye patches are not joined. The legs remain reddish but the bill becomes black. The juvenile is scaly on the upperparts, the mantle and wing coverts being white with a subterminal dark line and gingery fringe. The ear coverts are dark. Rest of cap is gingery brown. No black bar across inner wing coverts as in Common Tern.

Voice Calls include a 'kit-kit-kit', a 'kyarr' and a diagnostic 'tzaa-ap', more nasal than other terns.

Habitat Freshwater marshes, especially those bordering lakes.

Food Flying insects, especially dragonflies and caddis flies. Also takes fish and other small marine creatures picked from water surface.

Range Breeds in North America from Alberta to Saskatchewan and Manitoba south to southern California, Colorado and Michigan. Also breeds, though less commonly, along the Atlantic coast from Long Island south to North Carolina and on salt marshes along the Gulf coast in Texas and Louisiana.

Movements Some birds moving down Atlantic coast of USA have drifted to Europe, with the first British record as recent as 1980. There have since been around 20 sightings of this species in Britain and Ireland. This spate of observations could be linked with its recent northward spread in the USA, coupled with increased observer awareness.

Forster's Tern in summer plumage. Similarities between Forster's Tern and the Common Tern cause problems of identification on both sides of the Atlantic. They are easier to separate in their winter rather than summer plumage.

Bridled Tern

Sterna anaethetus 36–38cm (14–15in)

Nest Shallow scrape in sand; sometimes on hard ground
Egg clutch One
Egg colour Pale buff to cream, with fine dark brown or red-brown speckles, spots and blotches
Laid May to June
Incubation 28–30 days
Fledging 55–63 days

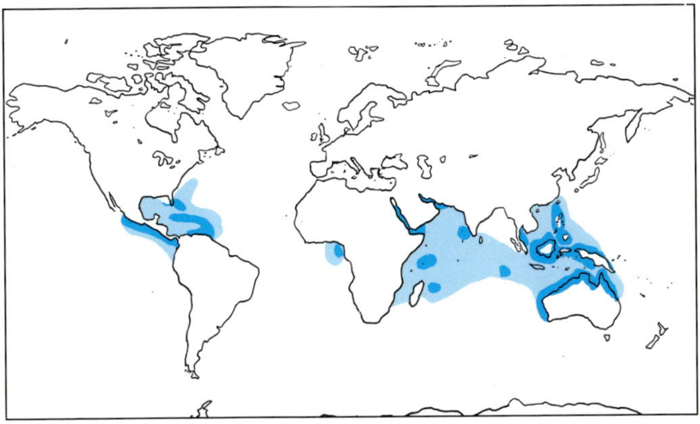

Identification Slightly smaller and slimmer than Sooty Tern which it resembles in adult plumage. Browner upperparts than Sooty Tern but also white underneath; there is a black cap with a white forehead extending over and behind the eye forming a supercilium. There is a white collar between the brownish-grey back and dark cap which can be difficult to see. Wings more pointed than Sooty Tern, with underwings and tail edges more extensively white; tail greyer. Sexes similar, no seasonal variation.

The juvenile bird resembles adult but cap is streaky while body upperparts brownish grey, tipped with buff and white, giving a mottled appearance.

Voice A harsh yapping 'wap-wap' or 'wrep-wrep'.

Habitat Tropical and sub-tropical waters nesting on sand and coral beaches. Normally frequents inshore waters usually returning to roost on land at night.

Food Small fish, crustaceans.

Range Breeds Caribbean, West Africa, Red Sea, Persian Gulf, Indian and Pacific Oceans.

Movements Disperses throughout breeding range after nesting. A vagrant to Europe, all sightings in Britain have been during the months of April to October. More recent records include an inland occurrence at Rutland Water in Leicestershire in 1984.

An adult Bridled Tern resembles the slightly larger Sooty Tern.

Sooty Tern

Sterna fuscata 41–45cm (17–18in)

Nest	Scrape in sand or on hard bare ground, occasionally adds bits of stick or grass round rim
Egg clutch	One
Egg colour	Cream covered irregularly with bright reddish-brown markings
Laid	May
Incubation	26 days
Fledging	30–36 days

Identification About the size of a Sandwich Tern and slightly larger than Bridled Tern, the adult Sooty Tern has markedly contrasting plumage, being black above and white below. Has a white forehead but lacks the white collar of Bridled Tern. There is a deeply forked tail and the underwing is distinctly two-toned along its full length. Sexes similar, no seasonal variation. A

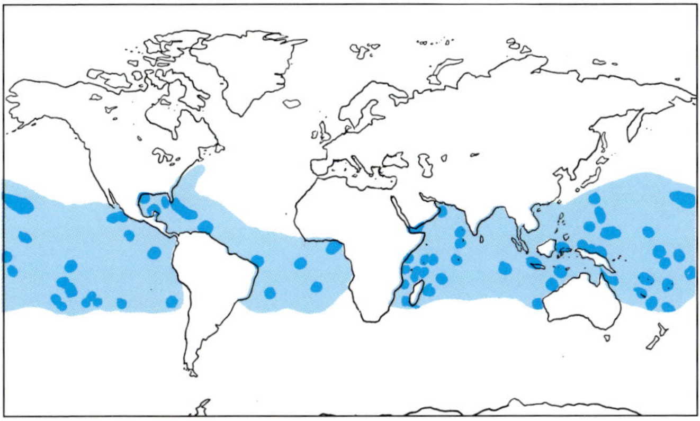

highly gregarious species which gathers in large numbers over shoaling fish. Obtains prey by catching fish from surface of the water while in flight: feeds during both day and night. Does not come to land except when breeding and is believed to sleep on the wing. Rarely settles on water. The juvenile is sooty brown overall with whitish stippling on the back; has a pale lower belly and undertail coverts; also has pale wing linings.

Voice Flight call 'keeer-wacky-wack' or 'wide-a-wake' from which bird gets the alternative name of Wideawake Tern. Has various other croaking alarm notes.

Habitat Tropical and sub-tropical seas, nesting on offshore and inshore islands.

Food Small fish and squid, taken from surface; does not dive for food like other terns.

Range Breeds on tropical and subtropical islands in all oceans and Red Sea.

Movements After breeding, generally disperses at sea in same region. The occurrences of this tropical tern in UK waters are scarce and have invariably been dead or dying birds, usually during the period May to August. Has been noted about a dozen times in Britain since 1958, the origins of which are speculative but are possibly hurricane-assisted Caribbean birds.

The Sooty Tern is blackish above and white below, lacking the white collar of the Bridled Tern, while the deeply forked tail is edged white.

Little Tern

Sterna albifrons 20–28cm (8–11in)

Nest A scrape in sand or shingle
Egg clutch Two
Egg colour Pale stone-green or blue with light brown blotches
Laid May to June
Incubation 22 days
Fledging 28 days

Identification Smallest of the terns, in breeding plumage has white underparts, being grey on the back and wings with black cap and a white forehead. The bill is sharply pointed, yellow with a black tip; feet are also yellow. Underparts are white. Flies with rapidly beating wings above the sea, sometimes rising vertically

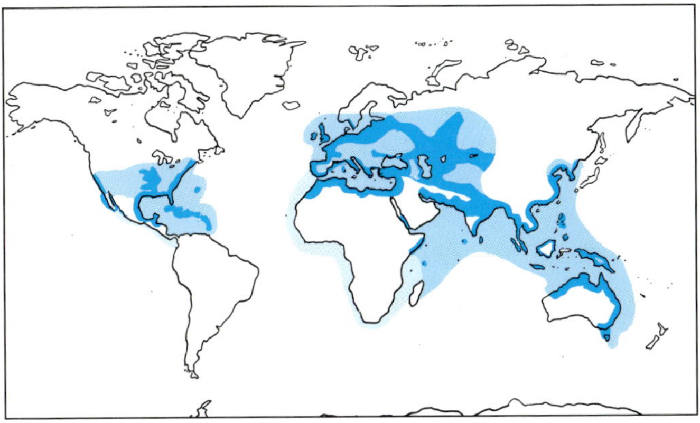

and stopping momentarily to hover head-on to the wind before plunging into the waves. When in flight a distinctive black wedge can be seen on the outer primaries. The tail is short but deeply forked. Juvenile is a pinkish-buff colour with brownish 'U'-shaped marking on feathers of upperparts. The crown is dusky and there is a dark mark on the ear coverts and a dark shoulder bar. First-summer birds are like adults but have dark bill and legs, shoulder bar, dark line through eye and dusky primaries.
Voice A high rasping 'kree-ik' or sharp repeated 'kitt', at times a harsh chattering 'kirri-kirri-kirri'.
Habitat Coastal, preferring shingle or sandy areas, but also found on rivers and some inland lakes where suitable conditions exist. There is great concern for the breeding population of the Little Tern as their seaside nesting sites are increasingly threatened.
Food Small fish and invertebrates, especially crustaceans, also insects.
Range A cosmopolitan species, there are eight subspecies. In Europe the nominate race (*S. a. albifrons*) breeds from British Isles and southern Baltic south to Mediterranean basin and from Morocco eastwards to Nile delta, Asia and north-west India.
Movements After nesting, birds move to winter in Central America southwards.

A Little Tern at its nest site, typically here on shingle.

Whiskered Tern

Chlidonias hybridus 25–26cm (10–10¼in)

Nest	An untidy platform of broken or uprooted sedges or rushes, generally larger than that of Black Tern and flimsier, heaped rather than woven
Egg clutch	Three
Egg colour	Light bluish-green, or pale yellowish-brown to cream, blotched black or brown
Laid	May to June
Incubation	18–21 days
Fledging	21 days

Identification Largest of the 'marsh' (*Chlidonias*) terns, it looks bulkier and has larger wings than either the other two *Chlidonias* species. However, it behaves more like a Sternidae, and in breeding plumage shows certain similarities with Arctic Tern. However, at such times it looks paler than the other marsh

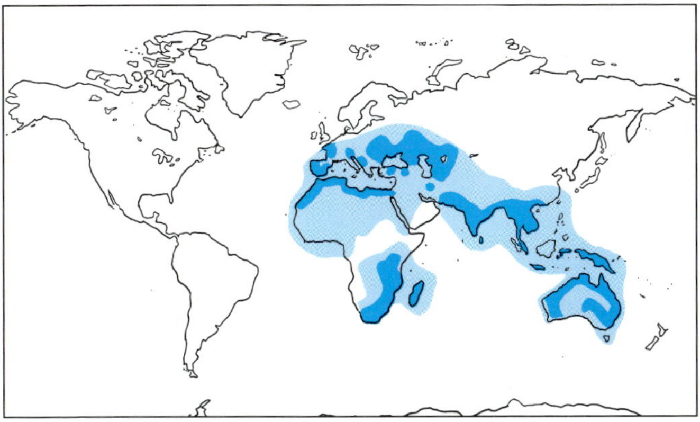

terns but shows a distinct black cap extending down the nape. This contrasts with the white face and dark grey underparts which at a distance give a distinct 'whiskered' look from which the bird gets its name. The underparts are ash-grey while the vent, undertail coverts and underwing are white. The tail is slightly forked while bill and legs are dull red. Flies in a leisurely style, plunge diving for food. The juvenile has a white forehead and pale cap. The upperwing is pale with no dark carpal bar, while the leading edge is pale. Care is needed in separating this species from Black Tern in non-breeding plumage.
Voice A rasping 'kyick' or 'cherk' at nesting locations, generally silent at other times.
Habitat For nesting, favours fresh water, marshland and areas of scattered pools.
Food Mainly insects and their larvae, especially dragonflies and beetles. Eats locusts and grasshoppers in winter quarters.
Range The nominate race breeds locally in southern Europe and northern Africa from Spain to Morocco and discontinuously eastwards through the Balkans and Tunisia to south-west Asia. There are other races breeding in South Africa and Madagascar from Kenya south to Tanzania, from Iran to India and in southern China, Taiwan, Indochina, Sri Lanka, Malaysia, Java, Celebes, Moluccas, New Guinea and Australia.
Movements After nesting, European breeding birds pass through Suez and Mediterranean and winter south to Africa.

A pair of Whiskered Terns at their nest, a floating platform of aquatic vegetation.

Black Tern

Chlidonias niger 22–24cm ($8^1/_2$–$9^1/_2$in)

Nest	Usually a heap of floating vegetation lined with fine stems. Occasionally a thinly lined scrape on dry ground
Egg clutch	Three
Egg colour	Brownish, greenish, blotched dark brown
Laid	May or early June
Incubation	14–17 days
Fledging	19–25 days

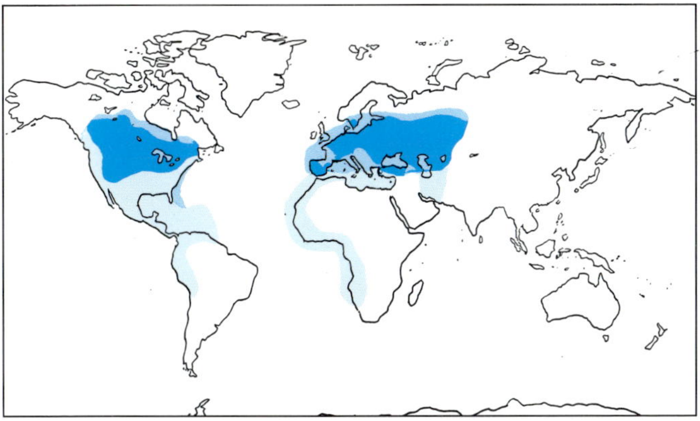

Identification A small tern, unmistakable in breeding plumage, being dark slate-grey all over, except for white undertail coverts which are most conspicuous and contrast markedly with dark body. The bill is black and the legs dark red. Flutters, dives and swoops above surface of water in characteristic 'marsh-tern' (*Chlidonias*) manner as it hawks for food, only very occasionally plunge dives. As they moult into non-breeding plumage, they look mottled and patchy, and then no longer live up to their name, looking grey on back with white forehead, neck and underparts. There are small blackish patches on the sides of the breast in front of the wings. Immature birds are like adults in winter, but have a darker saddle on the back. In this plumage, not easy to differentiate from White-winged Black Tern, which is a casual vagrant to east coast.
Voice A weak 'kit-kit' or similar note.
Habitat For breeding, favours both fresh and brackish water with plenty of emergent vegetation, small pools, lakes, ditches, overgrown canals, quiet reaches of rivers, marshes and swampy meadows.
Food Chiefly aquatic insects and their larvae picked from surface, but will also take small fish, tadpoles and small frogs.
Range Breeds Europe and western Asia from Sweden and Spain eastwards to south-west Siberia and the Caspian Sea. Has bred in Britain.
Movements After nesting, dispersal begins in July, August and September when thousands pass westwards through the Strait of Gibraltar to winter mainly along coasts of Ghana and Nigeria. During spring and autumn passage many move through Britain when noted at inland reservoir sometimes in hundreds (especially in May if winds are from south-east).

White-winged Black Tern

Chlidonias leucopterus 22–24cm ($8^1/_2$–$9^1/_2$in)

Nest	A floating platform of water weed, though exceptionally, an unlined scrape on a dry shoreline
Egg clutch	Three
Egg colour	Cream to pale buff, with large black and brown spots and blotches
Laid	June
Incubation	18–22 days
Fledging	24–25 days

Identification Most elegant of the 'marsh' (*Chlidonias*) terns; unmistakable in breeding plumage when black head and body plumage contrast with its white tail coverts and forked tail. The bird's name is derived from the pattern of the wings which have blackish grey outer primaries shading to white on the lesser

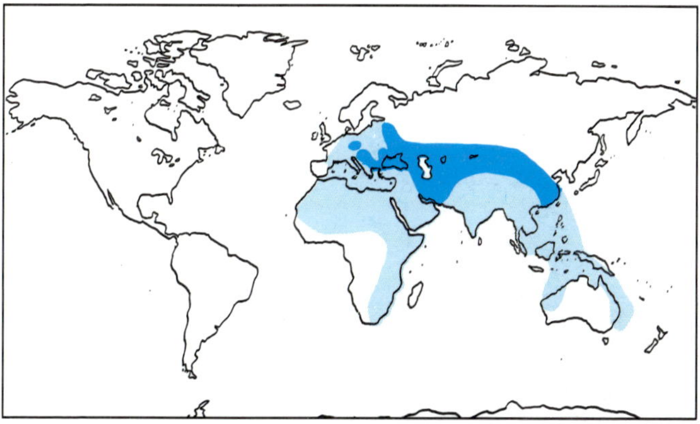

coverts. The underwing coverts are also black: a further distinguishing feature. The bill is black tipped with crimson, and the short legs are bright red. Skilful on the wing, dipping and wheeling and stalling just above the water when feeding. Readily lands in water, and at times may wade or walk in muddy areas. Will also catch insects in flight over land. The juvenile has a diagnostic combination of a dark saddle, pale mid-wing panel and a whitish rump. It has no dark mark at side of breast as does Black Tern. In autumn, some adults will show varying amounts of breeding plumage giving a patchy mottled appearance. In non-breeding plumage (usually complete by October) the adult is a pale grey-looking bird, resembling a Black Tern in winter, but differing principally in less extensive black cap and whitish, not grey, rump.

Voice On breeding grounds, utters a variety of harsh rattling and churring sounds; at other times generally silent.

Habitat At all times favours fresh water, such as flooded grassland or similar swampy conditions.

Food Small fish and various aquatic invertebrates.

Range In Europe breeds eastwards from Hungary with an uneven distribution across Asia to central Russia. There is a large gap in central Asia but further east it is to be found in southern China.

Movements A late migrant; does not arrive at nesting grounds much before end of May. After nesting, southward migration begins from August onwards. Most of the Eurasian population moves to central and southern Africa, passing along the Nile and the Rift Valley. Asian birds move to southern China, India, the Malay archipelago, Indonesia and northern Australia. A scarce but regular passage migrant in Britain.

An adult White-winged Black Tern in summer plumage.

Black Skimmer

Rhynchops niger 40–50cm (16–19½in)

Nest A simple scrape
Egg clutch Two to five
Egg colour Buff to blue-green, heavily blotched purplish black
Laid May to July
Incubation 23 days
Fledging 28 days

Identification An unmistakable bird with a distinctive feeding technique. In breeding plumage has a black crown, nape, hindneck, back and wings, while the forehead, face and underparts are white. The unique bill is bright vermilion with the terminal half of the upper mandible and most of the lower

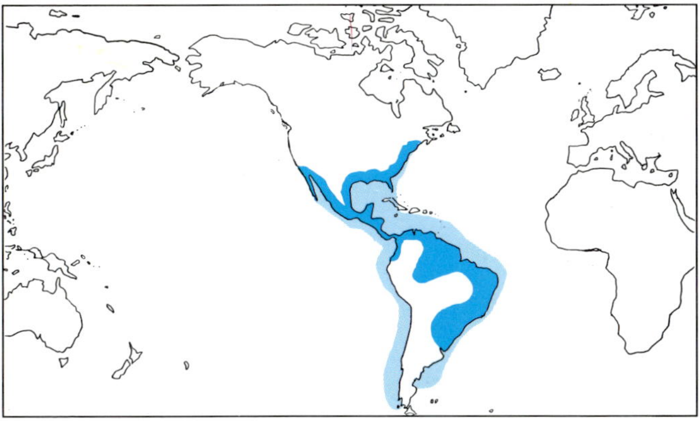

mandible black. The legs and feet are also bright vermilion. Despite spending long periods inactive, flocks of these birds perform bouts of synchronous flight, twisting and turning in unison. However it is when feeding that it reveals its special skill. At such times they fly straight and low over the water, beak wide open with the tip of the longer lower mandible ploughing the surface. When lower mandible strikes prey, the short-hinged upper mandible snaps down on it; at the same time the head is brought sharply backward and clear of water to swallow catch. The juvenile bird is mottled ginger-brown in the upperparts while the bill is dusky red with a blackish tip. Legs are dull red. In winter adults are slightly duller and have a white collar.
Voice During courtship, utters a series of drawn-out barking notes.
Habitat For nesting prefers broad sand bars, or large river systems or low coastal sandflats.
Food Fish, shrimps and other aquatic creatures obtained by its characteristic technique of skimming the water with longer lower mandible submerged.
Range Breeds locally along Atlantic coast south from Massachusetts, down through the Gulf coasts to northern Brazil. On the Pacific coast it breeds from north-west Mexico southwards to Ecuador. In California it now breeds Salton Sea and San Diego Bay area.
Movements After nesting, winters on the Pacific coast from San Diego Bay south to Chile. While on the Atlantic coast they are found southwards from the northern shores of the Gulf of Mexico and east Florida. Wind-blown individuals have occurred beyond the limits of their usual range.

Guillemot

Uria aalge 42–43cm (16–17in)

Nest	Bare rock ledge
Egg clutch	One
Egg colour	Creamy white to pale or deep blue-green to buff, blotched brown or black
Laid	Mid-May
Incubation	28–37 days
Fledging	15–17 days

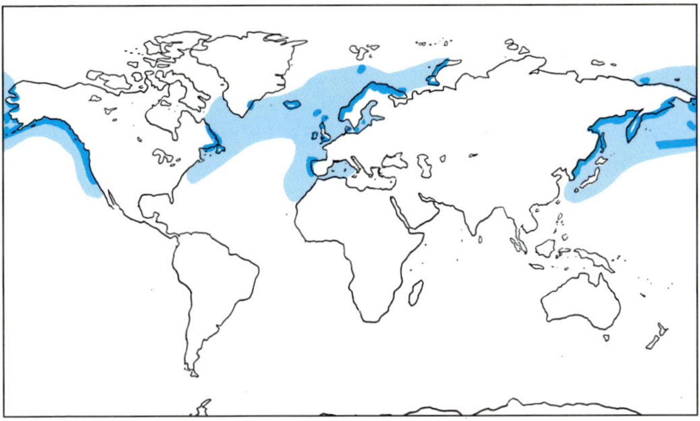

Identification Probably the most familiar of the North Atlantic auks, it might however be confused with Razorbill. Basically black and white in appearance, close views reveal the head and neck are dark chocolate-brown while the bill is long, slender and pointed. On the sea sits lower than Razorbill and tail is not cocked like that species. When diving for food can stay underwater for at least a minute. There is a so-called 'bridled' or 'spectacled' form: this is not a subspecies but a variant that has a white ring around its eye with a white line running back over the sides of the head. In more northerly latitudes the incidence of 'bridled' birds increases. In winter, loses much of the black around the head and neck with its chin, throat and cheeks becoming white with a dark, post-ocular stripe across the ear coverts. In its first winter the young Guillemot's head is darker, no stripe, and the bill is proportionately shorter.
Voice At nesting, colonies noisy with incessant cacophony of guttural wailing noises. At other times silent.
Habitat For nesting, steep precipitous rocky cliffs. At other times out to sea.
Food Chiefly fish, but some invertebrates taken.
Range Breeds Greenland to Norway, Faeroes, Orkney, Shetlands, British mainland, Baltic coast, north-west France, Portugal.
Movements After breeding, disperses to adjacent seas, but generally avoids deep oceanic waters.

A Guillemot in breeding plumage. The sharp, pointed bill helps distinguish it from the Razorbill with which it often shares breeding sites.

Brunnich's Guillemot

Uria lomvia 43–48cm (17–19in)

Nest	Bare rocky ledge of steep cliff faces
Egg clutch	One
Egg colour	Varies from creamy white to buff, patterned and blotched with brown
Laid	May to June
Incubation	30–35 days
Fledging	25 days

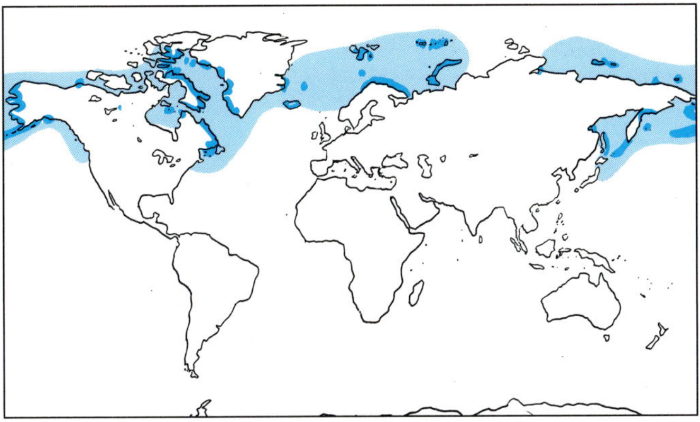

Identification An altogether darker bird than Guillemot, with upperparts and throat blacker-looking. The white underparts usually form a sharp point on the foreneck. It is slightly larger than the Razorbill with a shorter, thicker neck and a shorter, much thicker, bill which is its main identifying feature. Even at a distance it is obviously larger than a Guillemot's bill. At close range, a white line along the side of the bill might be seen, though it is absent in some birds. The face and neck of a non-breeding or immature bird is always darker than in Guillemot. First-summer birds are browner above than adults and retain much of winter plumage. In autumn, moulting birds can be confusing, but Brunnich's Guillemot retains breeding plumage (even into October).
Voice Highly vocal in breeding season, with calls similar to Guillemot.
Habitat For nesting, rocky precipitous cliff faces, at other times adjacent seas.
Food Mostly fish, but also some invertebrates taken.
Range Breeds from the Gulf of St Lawrence, Labrador and Hudson Bay in Canada to Greenland, Iceland, Jan Mayen, Spitsbergen, Franz Josef Land and Nova Zemlaya, USSR. Race *U. l. arra* breeds on Wrangel Island and along Chukchi Sea coast from Cape Lisburn south through Bering Sea to Aleutian Islands, Gulf of Alaska and Commander Islands. Some nest Cape Parry in Canadian North West Territories.
Movements Winters at sea adjacent to breeding areas with dispersal largely governed by presence of sea-ice. Rarely noted in British waters.

The Brunnich's Guillemot in summer plumage.

Razorbill

Alca torda 40–45cm (15½–17½in)

Nest	Bare rock, ledge or crevice
Egg clutch	One, rarely two
Egg colour	Greenish, white or light brown background patterned with brown blotches
Laid	May
Incubation	30 days
Fledging	14–21 days

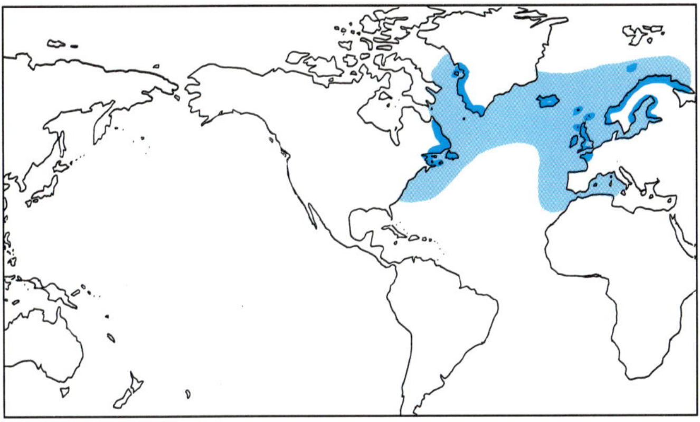

Identification Generally looks blacker than Guillemot and appears a more compact, plumper bird with thicker neck and heavier-looking head. The tail is longer and pointed and often cocked. On sea, dives with more of a splash than other auks, giving a distinct kick of the legs and a flick of the partly opened wings as it does. At close range, the laterally compressed bill crossed by a white line is a distinctive feature.

In non-breeding plumage, the adult is somewhat brown-looking, with the throat and face turning white. The juvenile is similar but the ear coverts and sides of breast are duskier. The bill is also slimmer and shows only an ill-defined white band.
Voice Various growling sounds at nest site, but otherwise generally silent at other times.
Habitat For nesting, rocky precipitous coasts; at other times adjacent seas.
Food Fish, with sand eels a major item.
Range Breeds Greenland, Iceland, Faeroes, British Isles, Ireland, Heligoland, Norway, Sweden, Finland and USSR. Restricted to north Atlantic, with nominate race breeding in North America from extreme south-eastern Baffin Island, Labrador coast, south-eastern Quebec, Newfoundland, north-eastern Nova Scotia, southern New Brunswick south to Grand Manau.
Movements After breeding, around the end of August, most European birds move to offshore waters in the North Sea. However some young birds move south to the Iberian peninsula, the western Mediterranean and Morocco.

The distinctive laterally compressed bill with its white lines, readily identify a summer-plumaged Razorbill.

Black Guillemot

Cepphus grylle 30–36cm (12–14in)

Nest	On bare ground in a crevice amongst boulders or scree, also a wide range of artificial sites used such as holes in harbour walls, under discarded fish boxes, under piles of driftwood
Egg clutch	Two
Egg colour	White-tinged cream, buff, blue-green, blotched black, brown grey
Laid	April to May
Incubation	28 days
Fledging	35–38 days

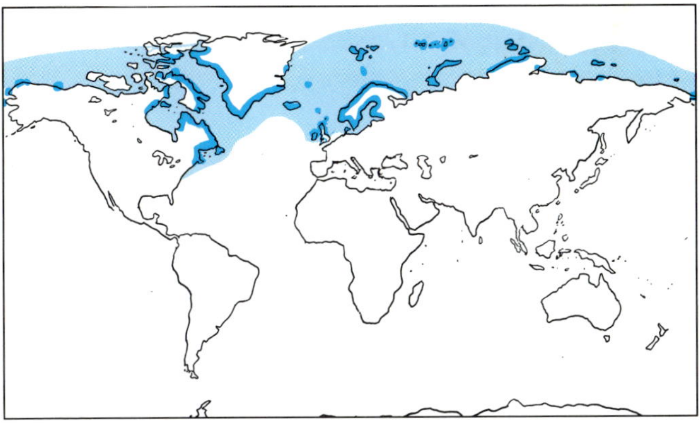

Identification An all-black bird except for large white patches on the wings. Red legs. Particularly striking in flight when black body contrasts with underwing of white bordered with black. Swims and dives as other auks but probably stays submerged longer. In non-breeding plumage looks quite different from late July onward when head and neck become predominately white. Furthermore, the white-fringed feathers of its upperparts give a heavily mottled appearance and the wing patch is much less distinct. The juvenile is similar to winter adult but is dusky on the crown and, at close range, the white wing patch shows a row of dusky spots.
Voice A whistling note during courtship and quite noisy at nest site. At sea and occasionally in flight, utters a shrill 'peeeee'.
Habitat Rocky and boulder-strewn coasts, particularly sea lochs and harbours, narrow inlets and fjords with relatively shallow water.
Food All manner of marine, but feeds more on crustaceans in the Arctic area of its range.
Range Has an almost circumpolar distribution. In north Atlantic breeds along High Arctic Canadian coasts, also North America, southern Greenland, Iceland, Faeroes, Sweden, Denmark, Norway, Murmansk and the White Sea. Also nests Britain and Ireland with concentration in Shetlands and Orkney.
Movements After breeding, disperses to adjacent waters. British birds are quite sedentary and spend most of winter months around or near the coastal areas where they nest.

Not so gregarious as other auks, the Black Guillemot is more likely to be seen singly or in small groups. Here a bird in summer plumage rests on a rock.

Little Auk

Alle alle 20–25cm (8–10in)

Nest	On ground, comprising a few small pebbles and occasionally a piece of lichen or straw
Egg clutch	One
Egg colour	Pale greenish-blue
Laid	June
Incubation	29 days
Fledging	28 days

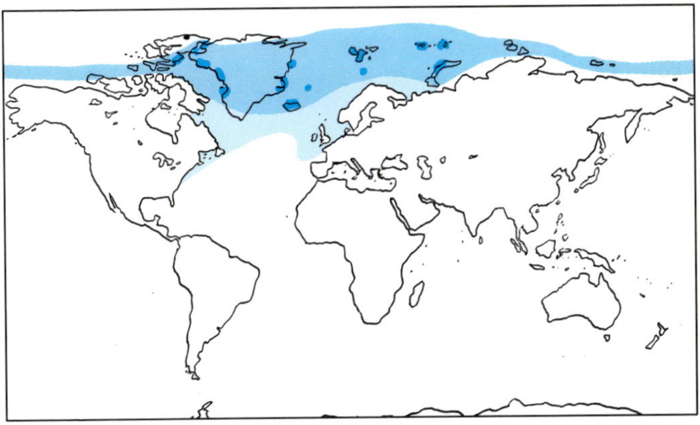

Identification A tiny seabird: in breeding plumage it is black above and white below, black upper breast contrasts sharply with pure white underparts. Non-breeding bird similar, except upper breast, throat and chin become white. Its small size, short stubby bill and appearance of having no neck should preclude confusion with other black and white alcids (auks). At close quarters, a distinctive feature is the white streaking on the scapulars. On land, sits upright on its tarsus like a tiny penguin, or squats full length on its breast as Puffins do. When on water sits very low. On the wing its fast, whirring flight is fairly distinctive, while the dark underwing should prevent confusion with juvenile Puffin or other similar plumaged auks, all of which have pale underwings. In winter ear coverts, throat and upper breast become white.

Juvenile plumage is similar to adults, though slightly browner.

Voice At breeding colonies, long trilling calls.

Habitat Mountain slopes of loose talus; rocks and scree from sea level to around 1500 feet; either facing or within easy flying distance of sea.

Food Mainly plankton, obtained in a series of shallow dives.

Range Breeds in High Arctic mainly nesting Greenland, Iceland, Norway, Zemlya, Spitsbergen and Jan Mayen. Also said to nest Ellesmere Island, Canada.

Movements After breeding, birds leave colonies and drift south with those moving into the North Sea, probably from Spitsbergen. In winter flights of hundreds, sometimes thousands, occur in Shetlands. Others noted down east coast as far south as Norfolk. Strong onshore winds occasionally wreck a number at inland locations.

Little Auks are winter visitors to British waters.

Puffin

Fratercula arctica 28–30cm (11–12in)

Nest	Underground chamber in old rabbit burrow excavated by birds. Can be under a pile of rocks. Lining is usually no more than a few bits of grass and feathers
Egg clutch	One
Egg colour	Dull white, with faint, grey reddish spots
Laid	May
Incubation	40 days
Fledging	38 days

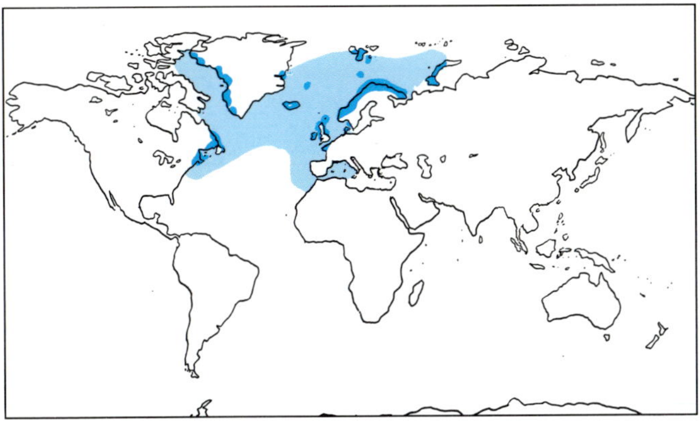

Identification Only Puffin of north Atlantic it is immediately identified by its massive brightly coloured red, yellow and blue beak. Upperparts black; underparts white, and face greyish white. The legs are orange red. After nesting, the colourful beak is lost along with the yellow rictal tubercles and other horny appendages round the eye. During the winter months the face of the adult looks a dirty grey, while the juvenile's is even darker, but with a smaller beak. At both ages the legs are dirty yellow in winter. On the sea, they swim easily, riding the waves in the roughest weather. Flight, low over the water, is rapid and whirring, and identification can be more of a problem. However, its more rounded wings, greyish wing linings and absence of a white trailing edge to the wing should help distinguish it from the Razorbill or Guillemot.
Voice Most vocal at nesting time when utters a low growling 'arr'.
Habitat For nesting, favours grassy islands and cliff tops.
Food Small fish, especially sand eels.
Range Breeds North America from Labrador to Maine, southern Greenland, Iceland, Norway, Sweden, Spitsbergen, Novaya Zemlya, Jan Mayen, British Isles and islands off north-west France.

In Britain, the major concentrations are to be found on Orkney, Shetlands and the western isles of Scotland. Also many scattered colonies round the western shores of Britain and Ireland. There is a notable population on the Farne Islands, Northumbria.
Movements After nesting, moves to adjacent offshore waters of the north Atlantic or Bay of Biscay.

Appendix

The following seabirds are irregular or scarce visitors to North American or European waters.

Yellow-nosed Albatross

Diomedea chlororhynchos
Length 71–81 cm (28–32 in)

A bird of the temperate and subtropical south Atlantic and Indian Ocean. It is considered unlikely to wander into the north Atlantic, but is very similar to the following species and might be wrongly identified. May also be confused with Black-browed Albatross, but is slimmer and longer-necked. The predominantly white underwing has a dark narrow border. Yellow ridge on top of adult's bill only visible at close range.

Grey-headed Albatross

Diomedea chrysostoma
Length 81 cm (32 in)

In distribution similar to above species and has been reliably identified about a dozen times on Atlantic coasts of North America. Much like Black-browed Albatross but can be separated by head, bill and underwing patterns.

Black-footed Albatross

Diomedea nigripes
Length 68–74 cm (27–29 in)

A north Pacific species, breeds Hawaii. Mostly dark in all plumages. White around bill and on undertail coverts more extensive in older birds but barely noticeable in immatures.

Wandering Albatross

Diomedea exulans
Length 107–135 cm (42–53 in)

Breeds Tristan da Cunha, Gough Island, also islands in Indian Ocean and off New Zealand. In Europe one record of a bird killed in Italy in 1957 and one seen off Portugal in 1963. Some other doubtful records. Most likely to be confused with Royal Albatross, but readily separable at most stages of plumage by progressive whitening of upperwing, with more white on older birds.

Laysan Albatross
Diomedea immutabilis
Length 81 cm (32 in)

Breeds on islands of the north Pacific. Its habit of colonizing aircraft runways, particularly on Midway, result in costly bird strike damage and many thousands of birds have been slaughtered in futile attempts at prevention. Regularly noted off the west coast of USA, though rare. Sometimes recorded inland in spring in south-eastern California. Quite numerous off Alaska. It has dark upperwing with white flash in primaries and white underwing showing irregular black markings making it fairly easy to identify. There are however, Black-footed Albatross *x* Laysan hybrids which pose an identification problem.

Capped Petrel
Pterodroma hasitata
Length 35–46 cm (14–18 in)

Breeds Hispaniola. European records comprise one found inland in Norfolk, 1852. A more recent record is of one long dead found in Yorkshire, December 1984. Has white forehead, white collar and white U-shaped band on rump. White wing linings show variable dark diagonal bar on leading edge, wing shape and white collar help separate from Great Shearwater.

Bulwer's Petrel
Bulweria bulwerii
Length 25–27 cm (10–10½ in)

Breeds Atlantic and Pacific oceans. Almost wholly black, with long, wedge-shaped tail and very fast, swooping flight. Three records off Britain and Ireland, the latest in 1975 off Cape Clear Island, Cork.

Little Shearwater
Puffinus assimilis
Length 25–30 cm (10–12 in)

Breeds islands of Atlantic, Pacific and Indian Oceans. North Atlantic population basically sedentary. Accidental around British waters with over 40 records in last 30 years. Resembles a Manx Shearwater, but is smaller and blacker above, with more white on face. Flight fast and whirring on very short wings. Seldom glides.

Audubon's Shearwater

Puffinus lherminieri

Length 30 cm (12 in)

Has a complex taxonomy and some authorities treat this species and Little Shearwater as conspecific. Also there are nine or ten subspecies. Has a rapid fluttering flight but not as fast as Little Shearwater. Occurs in Gulf Stream along Atlantic coast to North America. In September totals have peaked at 1500 birds off Virginia, where some remain until November. Noted as far north as New York.

Flesh-footed Shearwater

Puffinus carneipes

Length 50 cm (19½ in)

Larger than Short-tailed or Sooty Shearwater, entirely dark above and below except for paler flight feathers. At close quarters pale base to bill and pale legs can be seen. Breeds Australia and New Zealand. Winters in north Pacific and regularly seen July to December from British Columbia south to California.

Short-tailed Shearwater

Puffinus tenuirostris

Length 36 cm (14 in)

Very like Sooty Shearwater but much smaller and has shorter bill and steeper forehead. Wing linings generally more uniform in colour. Breeds south Australia, Tasmania, winters in north Pacific, when occurs along North American west coast from British Columbia to California. Some non-breeding birds present at other times. Used for food by early mariners when known as the 'mutton bird'.

Black-vented Shearwater

Puffinus opisthomelas

Length 36 cm (14 in)

Formerly considered to be subspecies of Manx Shearwater, it is dark brown above and white below with dark undertail coverts. There is variable dusky mottling at the sides of the breast, often extending right across. Breeds on islands of Baja California, dispersing north and south after nesting. Can often be seen from shore along Californian coast from August through to May.

Wilson's Petrel

Oceanites oceanicus
Length 15–19 cm (6–7½ in)

Breeds Antarctic and islands of southern oceans. Until 1985 only eight records in British waters, but in recent years many more have been observed off south-west Cornwall. Smaller than Leach's Petrel, skims over waves with shallow fluttering wing beats like a swallow. Wings short and rounded. Trails legs which extend beyond tip of tail. Yellow webbing between toes only visible at close range.

Fork-tailed Storm-Petrel

Oceanodroma furcata
Length 22 cm (8½ in)

Breeds from Kuril and Commander Isles through Aleutian chain east to Sanak Islands, also perhaps south-east coasts of Kamchatka. Also breeds southerly Alaska, Washington, Oregon, and northern California. Distinctively bluish grey above and pearl grey below. Shows dark grey forehead and eye patch, wing linings also dark. Wing beats rapid and shallow, often followed by long glide. Looks long-tailed in flight. Now rare off California coast but becomes more abundant further north.

White-faced Petrel

Pelagodroma marina
Length 20 cm (8 in)

Breeds in subtropical north Atlantic islands; also islands of southern oceans. Flies low over water with still, shallow wing beats interspersed with short glides. Has distinctive white underparts, wing linings and face. Has dark eye stripe, crown and underparts with a paler rump.

Ashy Storm-Petrel

Oceanodroma homochroa
Length 20 cm (8 in)

Grey brown overall, being darkest on crown, leading edge of wings and upper surface of flight feathers. Pale mottling on underwing only visible at close range. Looks long-tailed side-on. Flight fairly direct but wing beats fluttery and not as swallow-like as Wilson's Petrel. Breeds on islands off central and southern California, where fairly common, although rare in winter.

Black Storm-Petrel

Oceanodroma melania
Length 23 cm (9 in)

Largest of all the dark Storm-Petrels, it is blackish brown overall with pale bar on upper surface of the wing. The tail is forked and fairly long. Its flight is graceful with slow, deep wing beats. Breeds uncommonly off the coast of southern California and on both sides of the Baja Peninsula. Commonly to be seen off the southern California coast to Monterey from late summer through to autumn.

Least Storm-Petrel

Oceanodroma microsoma
Length 15 cm (6 in)

A tiny Storm-Petrel, appearing almost tailless in flight, which is indirect and low over the water with deep wing beats. Breeds only on islands of western Baja California and on northern islands in Gulf of California. Fairly common to abundant off coast of southern California in late summer and autumn.

Brown Booby

Sula leucogaster
Length 76 cm (30 in)

A dark brown bird, shows sharply contrasting white underparts and white wing linings. Male has whitish head and neck. Pantropical, it is possibly the most widespread Booby in east Pacific. There are four subspecies with *S. i. brewsteri* breeding in the Gulf of California south along Mexican mainland. Casual at Salton Sea and along Colorado River valley in late summer. Accidental along Atlantic coast to New Jersey (dark-headed eastern form). It is regular in the Gulf of Mexico and the Dry Tortugas.

Masked Booby

Sula dactylatra
Length 81 cm (32 in)

Distinguished from Gannet by yellow bill and extensive black facial skin, black tail and black secondaries. Immatures have yellowish bill, brown underparts with white on wing coverts. There is a white patch on the upper back and often a white collar. Breeds on islands of tropical oceans. In USA rarely seen from mainland but fairly common in Gulf of Mexico in summer and occasionally offshore to North California.

Dalmatian Pelican

Pelecanus crispus
Length 160–178 cm (63–70 in)

Very like the Great White Pelican (*P. oncocrotalus*), though usually slightly larger. In flight shows dusky secondaries and black wingtips above and all dirty white below. Now rare in southern Europe, breeding only Romania, Danube Delta, Greece, Albania, Turkey, USSR east to Chinese border and also possibly China, Mongolia and Iran.

Magnificent Frigatebird

Fregata magnificens
Length 102 cm (40 in)

One of five similar species of large dark predator seabird with long wings and long, forked tails, the male Magnificent Frigatebird is glossy black with an orange throat pouch that becomes bright red and inflated in courtship display. Breeds tropical and subtropical Atlantic and Pacific Oceans, also Marquesas Key of South Florida. Occasionally noted along both coasts. In Britain there have been three records since 1960.

Great Black-headed Gull

Larus ichthyaetus
Length 69 cm (27 in)

Breeds southern Russia and west and central Asia. Accidental in Britain but none since 1932. Between Herring Gull and Great Black-backed Gull in size, but structurally looks quite different to both, having the bulk of the latter and the longer, thinner-winged look of the former. In summer plumage the black hood and large, heavy bill are very obvious.

Slaty-backed Gull

Larus schistisagus
Length 64 cm (25 in)

A north-eastern Asiatic species. Adult has very dark grey back and wings with broad, white trailing edge, legs bright pink, eye yellow. Compare with Siberian form of Herring Gull, *L. a. vagae*, which is widespread in western Alaska.

Thayer's Gull

Larus thayeri

Length 59 cm (23 in)

Primarily a coastal species, but frequents large lakes or rivers, as well as rubbish tips and sewage outfalls. Breeds Arctic Canada and Greenland from Banks Island east to Puffin Island, and south to the Kent Peninsula and Southampton Island. Dispersal after breeding begins in August with main wintering areas being the west coast in British Columbia and Washington with smaller numbers found south to central Baja California. It is less commonly found north to Alaska. In the east occurs rarely around Gulf of St Lawrence and the eastern Great Lakes. In size and shape recalls Iceland Gull, despite the fact that the bill is slightly larger and head slightly more angular.

Elegant Tern

Sterna elegans

Length 40–43 cm (16–17 in)

Breeds California and western Mexico. Bill larger and thinner than Royal Tern with colour ranging from reddish orange in adults to yellow in some juveniles.

Aleutian Tern

Sterna aleutica

Length 33–38 cm (13–15 in)

Breeds Alaska and extreme north-east USSR. Only one western Palearctic record in the Farne Islands, 1979. Dark grey above and below. Has white forehead and black cap, black bill and black legs. Shorter tail, white forehead and dark, white-edged bar along one edge of secondaries help distinguish it from Common or Arctic Terns.

White-cheeked Tern

Sterna repressa

Length 35 cm (14 in)

An adult summer-plumaged bird was identified at Dungeness, Kent in May 1989, the first record (yet to be ratified by the BOU) for this species anywhere in Europe. Breeds north-west Indian Ocean, Red Sea from Gulf of Suez, Gulf of Aden, Somali and Persian Gulf east to Malabar coast, western India; also in East Africa south to Kenya.

Ancient Murrelet

Synthliboramphus antiquus
Length 25 cm (10 in)

Black crown and nape contrast with grey back. White streaking on head and nape in breeding plumage give it 'ancient' look and name. Chin and throat black, yellowish bill. Less black under chin in winter. Breeds Commander Islands and Kamchatka through Kurile Islands to Korea, and from Aleutians eastward to Alaska and British Columbia. There are about 40 Alaskan colonies of an estimated 400,000 birds. Winters as far south as California.

A bird off Lundy, Pembrokeshire in 1990 was the first record for Western Palearctic.

Least Auklet

Aethia pusilla
Length 16 cm (6½ in)

Smallest of all alcids, it is sooty black above with underparts variable, heavily mottled with grey or nearly all white. The stubby bill is dark red with a pale tip. Close views show the forehead and lores to be streaked with white bristly feathers. In summer plumage a streak of white plumes extend back from the eye. In winter the underparts are entirely white. Juvenile resembles non-breeding adult. Nests on boulder-strewn beaches and islands in countless numbers. Alaskan population estimated at 6 million. Winters mainly within breeding range.

Glossary

Axillaries The feathers at the base of the underside of the wing – in the armpit of the bird.
Carpel joint The bend of the wing – the small bones of the 'wrist' in a bird's wing.
Circumpolar Found either around the North or South Pole.
Concolorous Of uniform colour.
Conspecific Belonging to the same species.
Coverts Small feathers overlying the base of primary, secondary and tertiary feathers.
Filoplumes Hair-like feathers.
Gape The angle formed by the lower border of the upper jaw and the upper border of the lower jaw created when the bill is opened.
Gonys The prominent ridge formed by the fusion of the two halves of the lower mandible towards the tip of the bill. Most evident in gulls.
Gular pouch Pertaining to the throat.
Intermediates Plumage condition of a species of bird when not totally recognizable as distinctive form which exists within that species, e.g. Fulmar.
Lores The area between the base of the upper mandible and the eye, on each side of the head.
Mandible The jaw.
Mantle The plumage on the back and folded wings.
Morph Denotes any one of the different colour forms of a species' population.
Nape The back of the neck.
Omnivorous Eating any sort of food indiscriminately.
Pelagic Living or occurring on the surface of the ocean.
Primaries The outer flight feathers of a bird's wing.
Rictal tubercles Knob-like projections around the base of the bill.
Rump Immediately above the uppertail coverts.
Scapulars The feathers which cover the shoulder area, where the upperwing joins the body.
Secondaries The inner flight feathers on the wing, located between the primary and tertiary feathers.
Subterminal band A band of colour almost at the end of the tail.
Supercilium A colour stripe running backwards, above the eye.
Tertials (or tertiaries) Small feathers at the upper 'arm', being the innermost secondaries.
Ventral Forming or belonging to the lower surface of the body.

UPPERWING

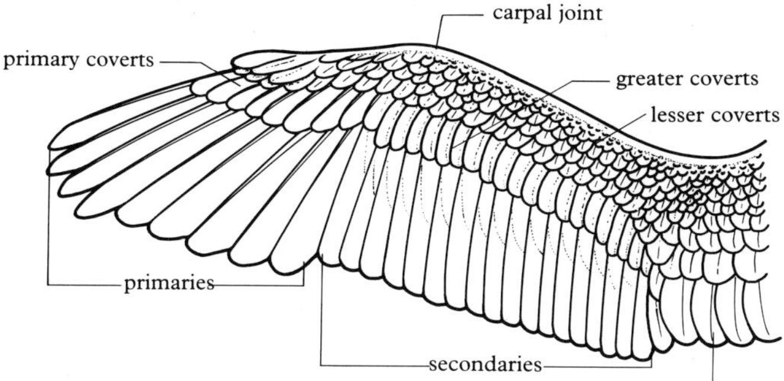
carpal joint
primary coverts
greater coverts
lesser coverts
primaries
secondaries
scapulars

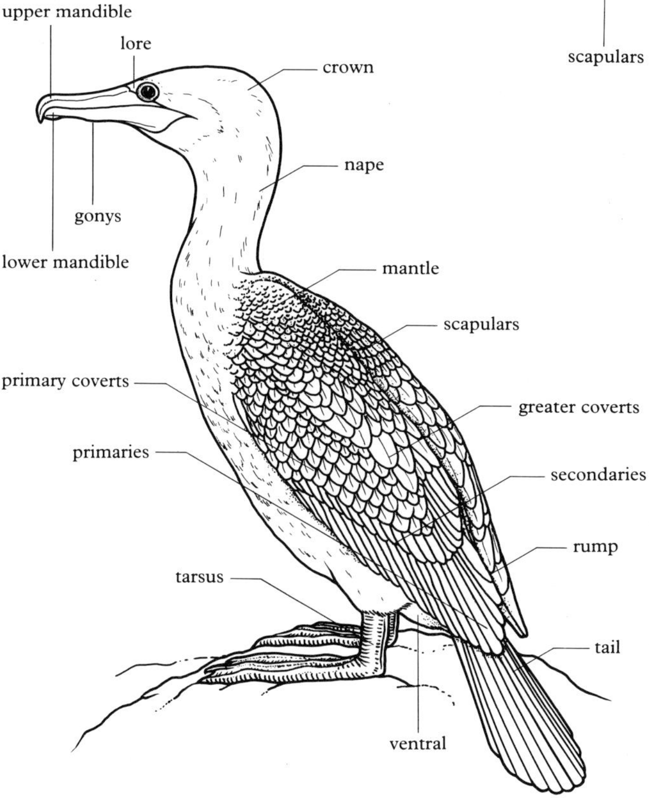
upper mandible
lore
crown
nape
gonys
lower mandible
mantle
scapulars
primary coverts
greater coverts
primaries
secondaries
rump
tarsus
tail
ventral

Bibliography

Cramp, S. and Simmons, K. E. L. (eds) (1987) *The Birds of the Western Palearctic* Vols I, III and IV. Oxford University Press, Oxford.

Dymond, J. N., Fraras, P. A. and Gantlett, S. J. M. (1987) *Rare Birds in Britain and Ireland.* Poyser, Calton.

Furnes, Robert W. (1987) *The Skuas.* Poyser, Calton.

Gooders, John. *Birds of the World*, Vols I to IX (Partwork) IPC, London.

Grant, P. J. (1986) *Gulls: A Guide to Identification*, Second Edition, Poyser, Calton.

Harrison, P. (1983) *Seabirds: An Identification Guide.* Christopher Helm, Bromley.

Harrison, P. (1987) *Seabirds of the World: A Photographic Guide.* Christopher Helm, Bromley.

Lack, Peter (ed.) (1986) *The Atlas of Wintering Birds in Britain and Ireland.* BTO, Irish Wildfowl Conservancy. Poyser, Calton.

National Geographical Society (1987) *Field Guide to the Birds of North America*, Second Edition. National Geographic Society, Washington.

Nettleship, David N. and Birkhead, Tim R. (1985) *The Atlantic Alcidae.* Academic Press, London.

Sharrock, J. T. R. (ed.) (1976) *The Atlas of Breeding Birds in Britain and Ireland.* BTO, Poyser, Berkhamsted.

Acknowledgments

I am grateful to the many photographers for the excellence of their illustrations. Their names are listed against the page number on which their photographs appear.

Front cover top: A. J. Bond; bottom: M. C. Wilkes;
Title page: A. J. Bond

8 P. Shaw
10 David D. Beadle
12 Paul Doherty
14 P. Harrison
16 S. Lasley/VIREO
18 G. W. Ward
20 D. A. Smith
22 S. Young
24 R. T. Mills
26 M. C. Wilkes
28 B. Hawkes
30 H. Kinloch
32 J. L. Roberts
34 W. Lankinen
36 M. C. Wilkes
38 C. Greaves
40 A. Frost
42 B. Hawkes
44 P. Mason
46 C. Hans Gebuis
48 M. C. Wilkes
50 W. Lankinen
52 S. Young
54 W. Lankinen
56 W. Lankinen
58 M. C. Wilkes
60 E. Mackrill
62 P. Harris
64 W. Lankinen
66 E. K. Thompson
68 M. Lane
70 S. C. Brown
72 N. Rodney Foster
74 B. Hawkes
76 R. Mellon/VIREO
78 E. K. Thompson
80 M. C. Wilkes
82 C. Hans Gebuis
84 R. Glover
86 M. C. Wilkes
88 M. C. Wilkes
90 B. Robson (Rare Bird Photographic Library)
92 B. Hawkes
94 R. T. Mills
96 D. S. Whitaker
98 R. T. Mills
100 R. Villani/VIREO
102 C. Greaves
104 Hanne & Jens Eriksen
106 M. C. Wilkes
108 J. J. Brooks
110 B. L. Sage
112 Hanne & Jens Eriksen
114 M. C. Wilkes
116 David D. Beadle
118 David D. Beadle
120 B. L. Sage
122 C. Heyes
124 E. K. Thompson
126 M. C. Wilkes

Index

Page numbers in **bold** refer to main description of bird

RSNC

The Royal Society for Nature Conservation is pleased to endorse these excellent, fully illustrated pocket guide books which provide invaluable information on the wildlife of Britain and Northern Europe. Royalties from each book sold will go to help the RSNC's network of 48 Wildlife Trusts and over 50 Urban Wildlife Groups, all working to protect rare and endangered wildlife and threatened habitats. The RSNC and the Wildlife Trusts have a combined membership of 184,000 and look after over 1800 nature reserves. If you would like to find out more please contact the RSNC, The Green, Whitham Park, Lincoln, LN5 7NR.
Telephone 0522 752326.